a Song for all seasons

Wilma Sullivan
with Pam Creason

AMBASSADOR-EMERALD INTERNATIONAL
GREENVILLE, SOUTH CAROLINA • BELFAST, NORTHERN IRELAND

A Song for All Seasons
Copyright © 1999 Wilma Sullivan

Published by
Ambassador-Emerald International
1 Chick Springs Road, Suite 203
Greenville, SC 29609 USA

and

Ambassador Productions
16 Hillview Avenue
Belfast, Northern Ireland
BT5 6JR

Cover design © 1999 Grand Design
Cover and internal design by Matt Donovan
Cover photography © 1999 Don Bishop/Artville

This book is dedicated to the One I love, Whom I love because He first loved me and gave Himself for me— my precious Lord and Savior, Jesus Christ.

"O magnify the LORD with me, and let us exalt his name together."

PSALM 34:3

Contents

Foreword

It has been my privilege to know Wilma Sullivan since 1985 when she first came to speak at our ladies' retreat in South St. Paul, Minnesota. Wilma lived in a house provided by our church when not traveling with her ministry responsibilities. And I was her pastor while she attended the church there. I have since come to know her as a personal friend and faithful servant of God.

I have seen Wilma go through the pain and glory of coming to know Christ as Lord of her life and ministry. I say pain because no one ever comes to know the reality of God without seeing the failure of self to live righteously and to serve Him effectively. All of our good intentions and works are worthless until Christ Himself becomes our very life. I have seen Wilma go through the pain and frustration of coming to this realization.

I have also observed Wilma as she has come to see something of the glory of Christian living and ministry. I say glory because that's what Christ brings into our lives when He reigns on the throne of our hearts. It is a life and ministry that honors Him because He is allowed to manifest His life in and through us. It is a life and ministry that seeks nothing for itself, but only for God.

I am thrilled to write the foreword for Wilma's book for several reasons. First, I believe the book helps to clarify what the Christian life really is. It is not the believer seeking to live for God and to serve Him in his own strength, but in the strength of the Lord. It is not living by rules and regulations, but by the indwelling presence of the Holy Spirit, who makes real and confirms to us the Word of God. Wilma's book makes this truth clear.

Secondly, I believe this book will be very encouraging to the reader. I was blessed and thrilled by the truth presented in each chapter. This book is very helpful to anyone wanting to know how to live the Christian life and to make his service acceptable to God. Wilma makes it evident from the Bible that there is a Christian life that really works!

Thirdly, I believe the book thoroughly and completely honors God and His Word, the Bible. If this were not the case, the book would have no real or eternal merit. I believe that what Wilma has to say as she discusses the truth of the Bible is in every way honoring to Him who is indeed our life (Colossians 3:4).

I heartily recommend this book to all who desire to enter into an intimate relationship with God, and who want to worship and serve Him in Spirit and truth.

Dr. Walter P. Olsen, Pastor
New Glarus Baptist Bible Church
New Glarus, Wisconsin

Introduction

I've always enjoyed a good song. I loved the songs my dad sang as a soloist in the Catholic church when I was a child as well as those that I sang with the nuns while I was in the convent. After that, I had fun singing with a musical summer theater group for a while, and I taught contemporary songs for the Masses in the Catholic church. But when I came to know the Lord Jesus Christ as my personal Savior on a November night in 1973, He did, as He said in Psalm 40:3, "put a new song in my mouth."

When I first approached the thought of "A Song For All Seasons," the Lord called my attention to Isaiah 12:2-5. "Behold, God is my salvation; I will trust, and not be afraid: for the LORD JEHOVAH is my strength and my song; He also is become my salvation. Therefore with joy shall ye draw water out of the wells of salvation. And in that day shall ye say, Praise the LORD, call upon His name, declare His doings among the people, make mention that His name is exalted. Sing unto the LORD; for He hath done excellent things: this is known in all the earth." Imagine that! My *God,* the LORD JEHOVAH, the I AM THAT I AM, *is* "my strength and *my song.*"

Continually discovering, exploring, and experiencing the rich treasures of the Lord keeps the divine melody stirring in my heart. What a joy it is to learn from God's Word the strains of God's mercy and grace which are always available and always sufficient for any "season"—any time and any need—in my life.

God desires that every one of us, as His children, enjoy an ever-deepening relationship of love with Him as we seek to know the Lord more fully. I still have much to learn as I keep seeking Him, but I would like to share some of the thoughts He has used to instruct me, encourage me, and bless my heart, especially in the last few years.

Christ longs to be our strength and song in every "season." Our hearts should beat with a cadence of praise, knowing that He will become our salvation right smack dab in the middle of our seasons, whatever they may be. My prayer is that the Lord might show you that Christ is your strength and your song in your seasons. He will set you free. You will be safe. You will have peace that passes all understanding to keep your heart and mind through Christ Jesus. May these themes that we are about the explore encourage a symphony of praise from your heart, and may God indeed be your song for all seasons.

At the close of each chapter you will find a "Selah Time" section. The word "Selah" occurs seventy-one times in the Psalms. Scholars think that it was probably some sort of musical direction for those singing the psalms or a signal for some particular act of worship to be conducted at that point. Some have also thought that it was an instructive phrase perhaps directing singers, readers, and hearers alike to "stop and think about that."

Our "Selah Times" ending each chapter will be opportunities for us to stop and think about what the Lord is teaching us in and through the seasons we are experiencing.

a Song for Spring

Spring is a time . . . of buds and blossoms bursting forth in their natural splendor; . . . of verdant pastures teeming with newborn calves and lambs; . . . of fresh and exhilarating experiences.

~

We may encounter the sensations of spring in our lives at one or many points in time . . . in marriage, in parenthood or perhaps in certain other events or achievements.

But there is no greater sense of new life to be found than that freely offered to us through the Lord Jesus Christ. Establishing that most important relationship with our Savior ushers in a vibrant season in our lives, a season intended to last for time and eternity.

~

Chapter 1

A SONG OF NEW BIRTH

Behold, God is my salvation; I will trust, and not be afraid: for the LORD JEHOVAH is my strength and my song; He also is become my salvation.

ISAIAH 12:2

Yes, God can and should be our song in any season of our lives. But before we can explore all the wonderful realities of that fact, there is a personal question that has to be answered. The Lord's strength and song come along with . . . never apart from . . . salvation. To know the riches of salvation through the Lord Jesus Christ is to know the fountain of life which can resonate through our lives in glorious song. Do you know Him as your salvation?

You may know that I am a former nun in the Catholic Church. I grew up in a good Catholic family. I wanted to serve God, and I thought the best way to do that was to become a nun. So, from 1967 to 1971, I was Sister Wilma Marie, R.S.M. (Religious Sisters of Mercy). I did choose to leave the convent after three and a half years, but not for lack of religious devotion or because I was angry or bitter with anybody. Rather, I grew disillusioned with the lifestyle of the nuns. When the problems that troubled me went unresolved, I simply left the convent in good favor and with an open invitation for return.

Though no longer a nun, I stayed intent on serving God actively in the Catholic Church. But despite my religious fervor as a nun and afterward, something critical in my standing before God had been missing all along. Then a hospital encounter in 1973 began to point me to that all-important reality of knowing God as my salvation.

While working as a secretary in a law firm north of Philadelphia, I was hospitalized for a problem with abdominal tumors. There in the hospital another patient, Lenore Dickinson, confronted me with the question, "If you would die in surgery today, do you know 100% for sure that you're going to go to heaven?" Knowing how I had tried to serve God all my life, I didn't think that there was any reason I wouldn't, so I responded that I did know for sure.

Lenore didn't leave it at that. She befriended me during the rest of my hospital stay and soon contacted me after we both had gone home. When she wanted me to come to her house and talk about spiritual things, I assumed that her medical problem was serious and that she wanted some counsel from her new ex-nun friend. I was glad to help.

After I had talked with her a while, two of her friends dropped by, and we all talked. They seemed interested to hear about my life. They also said that their pastor, who had been raised by nuns in an orphanage, would love to meet me. I think I shocked them when I told them I'd like to meet him.

The next Sunday, after going to Mass, I showed up at their Baptist church. I was impressed by the joyful singing and by the way everyone followed in the Bible as the pastor preached. For two weeks I became a fanatic Catholic and Baptist at the same time, faithfully attending Mass as well as all the services at that Baptist church. Then I made arrangements to talk to the pastor.

In his office, after a Sunday evening service on November 11, 1973, the pastor talked to me about what God had done in his life. He spoke of God's mercy and grace, and he told me that before he knew of God's salvation, he hadn't known that he was bad enough to go to hell just by being born into this world.

That thought stopped me dead in my tracks. I knew about the goodness of God. I knew about the love of God. And I knew about the service of God. But for the first time in my life, the reality of the justice and judgment of God caught my attention. He went on to explain that nothing takes away the penalty of sin but the blood of Jesus Christ.

That night, as that pastor related what the Bible says about sin and about how Christ died on the cross to save me, I came face to face with my need for salvation. I bowed my head there in his office and accepted the Lord Jesus as my personal Savior.

> Therefore being justified by faith, we have peace with
> God through our Lord Jesus Christ (Romans 5:1).

Shortly after my salvation, a man from Philadelphia named Alex Dunlap put my testimony into pamphlet form. The title is "Ex-Nun Finds Peace with God," and this verse, Romans 5:1, is on the front of the pamphlet. When I've handed it to people as a witness to them, many have looked at me and said, "You mean to tell me that you didn't have peace with God as a nun?" The answer to that question is no, I did not.

The reason lies in that verse, Romans 5:1. The Apostle Paul is making two points there. First of all, it says that we are "justified." In order for you and me to get to heaven, we must be justified. What does that mean? Let's put it simply: it means that you and I must be just like Jesus Christ in order to live with Him for all of eternity and to have power over sin in our lives every day. It means being declared righteous by God, made "just as if I'd never sinned" in His eyes.

The second point in that verse is about having "peace with God." How does he say we have that peace? Through our Lord Jesus Christ. Paul is drawing the conclusion by making this statement that peace with God isn't something that we are born with or that we acquire on our own. Why? Because it comes only through Jesus Christ.

So why don't we have peace with God? Let's start with the most popular verse in all of the Bible, John 3:16.

> For God so loved the world, that He gave His only
> begotten Son, that whosoever believeth in Him should
> not perish, but have everlasting life (John 3:16).

A Song for Spring

For God *so* loved—that word "so" is one of the smallest words in the English language, and yet we will never fully understand its meaning until we see Christ. God so loved the world that He gave His only begotten Son [the Lord Jesus] that whosoever believeth in Him [not do one other thing] should not perish [and go to hell] but have everlasting life [life that lasts forever!]. It's such a wonderful verse of love and promise, but that's not all. Let's continue on to the next two verses.

> For God sent not His Son into the world to condemn the world; but that the world through Him might be saved. He that believeth on Him is not condemned: but he that believeth not is condemned already, because he hath not believed in the name of the only begotten Son of God (John 3:17-18).

Jesus came that the world—each one of us—might be saved. He didn't come to call the righteous, but sinners to repentance (Matthew 9:13). He came to seek and to save that which was lost (Luke 19:10). We all need to be saved because we all qualify as lost sinners. Without Him we all stand already condemned and will perish, but by believing in Him we escape that condemnation. When Jesus said in verse 18 that a person who "believes" on Him is not condemned, that's believing not just in your head (intellectually) but in your heart (in your inner person). It's the word trust.

> He that believeth on the Son hath everlasting life: and he that believeth not the Son shall not see life; but the wrath of God abideth on him (John 3:36).

The wrath of God abides on us because we are all born in sin. Romans 5:12 explains, "Wherefore, as by one man sin entered into the world, and death by sin; and so death passed upon all men, for that all have sinned." That's what we call "original sin." We all have it, and it condemns us because a holy God cannot condone sin. When we look back at Romans 5:1, we can now understand why we don't have peace with God. All

6

of us have sinned and come short of the glory of God, and there is none righteous: no, not one (Romans 3:10, 23).

That's why we so desperately needed God to love us and give His Son so that we wouldn't have to perish. Christ had to come and die to take away our sins with His precious blood. Romans 5:8 says, "But God commendeth His love toward us, in that, while we were yet sinners, Christ died for us." He didn't wait for us to clean up our lives first. He already demonstrated His love for us by the sacrifice of Jesus Christ. Romans 6:23 says, "For the wages of sin is death," and as my Catholic Bible puts it, "the free gift of God is eternal life in Christ Jesus our Lord."

When we accept that free gift, we become "justified," made "just like Jesus Christ" and now have eternal life. When we are justified, we have a position in God's eyes of being "just as if we never sinned," and we are then righteous in His eyes because the righteousness of Jesus Christ is imputed or attributed to us. We can have that right standing with God, not because of anything we have done, but because of what Christ has done for us.

> Much more then, being now justified by His blood, we shall be saved from wrath through Him (Romans 5:9).

We have God's wrath on us when we are born into this world, but Jesus Christ came to die in our place to wash away our sins by His precious blood. And as that pastor explained to me on that November night, there is nothing that can take away our sins except the blood of Jesus Christ.

Look at that verse again. "Being *now* justified . . ." You don't have to wait to find out if you're going to heaven when you die. No, you can know right now by claiming His promises and depending on His faithfulness. All you have to do is to believe it and trust in the fact that He died for you personally. Call upon His precious Name, and you will be justified—made "just as if you had never sinned."

> For by grace are ye saved through faith; and that not of yourselves: it is the gift of God: Not of works, lest any man should boast (Ephesians 2:8-9).

I am so thankful that I was taught by the priests and nuns while I was growing up about Jesus Christ: that He was born of Mary the Virgin; that He lived here on the earth approximately thirty-three years; that He died on the cross for the sins of the whole world; that three days later He arose from the grave physically; that He stayed here 40 days to prove that He had risen from the dead; and that He then ascended into heaven and is now seated at the right hand of the Father interceding for us day and night. I was told that I had to believe all of that (and I believe it even more now), but I also was told that I had to do several things to help me get to heaven. But Ephesians 2:8-9 clearly states that "doing things" isn't a part of salvation at all. The night I was saved, I found out that I didn't have to do anything, but that "Jesus paid it all, All to Him I owe; Sin had left a crimson stain, He washed it white as snow." How did He do that? With His precious blood.

Several years ago I was staying with an artist in Colorado. Her name was Ardie, and she patterned some of her work after that of Bob Ross, a professional painter who had a program on TV. After watching his program one day, we turned off the TV and began talking about colors—what color mixed with what color makes what color? Making an observation, Ardie said, "Wilma, you have a red blouse on. How about if we take a red light bulb and put it in this lamp, turn it on, and shine it down on your red blouse. Do you know what color you would see?"

I said, "red."

She said, "No, Wilma. You'd see white!"

Immediately the spiritual application hit home. I'm born with dirty blood and so are you. All of us are born in sin. But Jesus Christ died on Calvary's cross and shed His precious blood as the Lamb of God for our sins. The night that I called upon the name of the Lord Jesus and asked Him to save me, I know He did, because I claimed His promise to me in Romans 10:13. "For whosoever shall call upon the name of the LORD *shall be* saved" [not I think, I hope, or I may be]. When I did that, He took His blood and He put it on top of mine. When God the Father looks through both colors of red, what color

does He see? "White!" He sees purity. He sees me justified—
"just as if I'd never sinned."

> That which is born of the flesh is flesh; and that
> which is born of the Spirit is spirit. Marvel not that I
> said unto thee, Ye must be born again (John 3:6-7).

In John chapter 3, Jesus speaks of salvation as our need to
be "born again" or "born from above." It is a "new birth" when
we believe in Christ, and God gives us eternal life. On April 2,
1944, I got a birth certificate. That's when I had my fleshly birth,
and you know when you had yours. But Jesus said we must
have the "second birth," to be born of the Spirit, the birth that
passes us from condemnation and death into life (John. 5:24).

Do you have the blood applied? Do you know the Lord
Jesus Christ as your salvation? Is He your song of new birth? If
your answer is no, I pray that you will experience that new birth
without delay. Please turn right now to the back of this book
and read page 137. There you will find further information
about how you can receive Christ as your personal Savior.

If you have experienced the new birth, aren't you glad that
Jesus is the Lamb of God and that He came to take away the sin
of the world? Aren't you glad that through the Lord Jesus Christ
you can have "peace with God!" What a joy it is to know Him as
your song of salvation!

NOTHING BUT THE BLOOD

What can wash away my sin? Nothing but the blood of Jesus;
What can make me whole again? Nothing but the blood of Jesus.

Nothing can for sin atone—Nothing but the blood of Jesus;
Naught of good that I have done—Nothing but the blood of Jesus.

This is all my hope and peace—Nothing but the blood of Jesus;
This is all my righteousness—Nothing but the blood of Jesus;

Oh! precious is the flow That makes me white as snow;
No other fount I know, Nothing but the blood of Jesus.

Robert Lowry (1876)

selah time

1. Think about what it really means to have peace with God. Do you have peace with God?

2. Look up Galatians 2:16. What can't justify us? What can justify us?

3. Do you have the new birth that Jesus talked about in John 3:6-7? If you are not sure, please read or reread pages 8 and 9.

Chapter 2

A SONG OF NEW LIFE

O sing unto the LORD a new song:
sing unto the LORD, all the earth.
Sing unto the LORD, bless His name;
shew forth His salvation from day to day.

PSALM 96:1-2

The new birth does indeed give us a new song because the Lord, as our salvation, becomes our song. But in addition, it gives us new life. The Lord said in John 10:10 that He came that we "might have life, and that [we] might have it more abundantly," and that abundant new life is exactly what becomes ours at the point of our new birth.

Many Christians, however, never learn what their new life is all about. And if they don't know, they can't live in the light of all its assurances and the availability of all its resources. Unfortunately, the result is usually Christian lives that are, well, "lifeless."

I pray that this exploration of our new life will encourage you with a refreshing look at some truths from God's Word. We'll examine many aspects of this new life more closely in later chapters, but for now we'll touch on a few of the important realities of our salvation.

For ye are dead, and your life is hid with Christ in God. When Christ, who is our life, shall appear, then shall ye also appear with Him in glory (Colossians 3:3-4).

Before we were saved we were dead spiritually. Ephesians 2:1 says, "You hath He quickened [made alive], *who were dead in trespasses and sins.*" So we were dead, but now Colossians 3:3 tells us that we are still dead. How can this be? We know that Christ made us alive at salvation, but He didn't give us "our own life." He gave us *His life.* He became our life!

That Christ is our life is an astounding reality with wonderful implications. Our Lord Jesus desires to live His life in and through us. But there is a problem. We take possession of His life once and for all at salvation, but allowing Him to live it in us and through us is a day-by-day, moment-by-moment decision on our part. We must constantly choose to allow His life to be seen in us.

Because Christ's life is indeed ours, we can potentially live all the time with His strength, His love, His peace, His patience, His goodness, etc. But let's be real. That just doesn't happen, does it? And why doesn't it? Because we keep trying to breathe life into that old corpse that we still hang on to as "our life," rather than claim the new life that is ours.

In the "strength" of "our life," we try and try to live with love and peace and patience and goodness, etc., but it doesn't work. When we falter or fall flat on our faces, we may cry out in prayer for God to "help us." But in doing so, we fail to recognize that dead people don't need help; they need life!

And life is exactly what we do have in Christ, but we ignore it or, all too often, we are totally ignorant of it. We go on, stumbling in our own strength, relying on our self-discipline to live the Christian life. When we have some apparent success, we pat ourselves on the backs for being "good." When we fail, we call out to God for His "help" and go on trying to muddle through, or sometimes we even give up in guilt and despair over our lack of self-control that let us be so "bad." The right choice doesn't involve self-discipline. On the contrary, it is a choice of death to self. It is a choice that allows us to claim the power of Christ's life in us.

For if, when we were enemies, we were reconciled to
God by the death of His Son, much more, being reconciled, we shall be saved by His life (Romans 5:10).

So much more! Salvation isn't just an escape from the penalty
of our sins, though we certainly should be thankful for that freedom. It's also the promise of "His life" to give us victory over the
power of sin in our daily walk. There is power in the blood of
Christ, and it has given us the sure hope of heaven in our future,
but it's no less powerful in the nasty now-and-now where the rub-
ber meets the road—today, right where you and I are!

From the point of our new birth until we see Him in glory,
we aren't left with crumbs of "help" from above to deal with sin
which so easily besets us. "Being reconciled, we shall be saved
[an on-going deliverance from the power of sin] by His [resur-
rection] life!"

In I Corinthians 15:3-4 we find the clear definition of the
gospel: "that Christ died for our sins according to the scriptures;
And that He was buried, and that He rose again the third day
according to the scriptures." Jesus did die on the cross and was
buried so that we could have our sins forgiven. He had to pay
the wages of our sin, and that was death. But for us who know
Jesus Christ as our personal Savior, the good news (the gospel)
now comes to focus on the third part—"that He rose again"
from the dead. He had victory over every sin so that we don't
have to live in it. We can claim the power of His resurrection life!

That I may know Him, and the power of His resurrection, and the fellowship of His sufferings, being made
conformable unto His death (Philippians 3:10).

The only way, however, we are going to learn about the
power of His resurrection in us is for us to get to know Him.
With the Apostle Paul, we should have that deep longing to
have our acquaintance with our Savior become more and more
intimate as we grow in our understanding of who He is. How
can we let the precious One, who is our life, continue to be
almost a stranger, little more than a passing acquaintance to us?

No woman would expect to have a good and fulfilling marriage if her relationship consisted of a few glimpses of her husband on certain days, performing some required tasks for him, and giving him "honey-do" lists now and then. Yet, so often we seem to settle for this kind of relationship with the One who has given us His very life. We catch a few glimpses of Him in some sermons or Bible readings, but we hurry on, and He's soon forgotten in our busy schedules. We try to do the things that we think are on His list of requirements for a spiritual Christian, and we hope that makes Him happy even though they are sometimes a burden to us. And, when we have a problem that we can't handle on our own, we let Him know that we'd like Him to step in and fix it. That's just not "knowing Him."

> Thus saith the LORD, Let not the wise man glory in his wisdom, neither let the mighty man glory in his might, let not the rich man glory in his riches: But let him that glorieth glory in this, *that he understandeth and knoweth Me,* that I am the LORD which exercise lovingkindness, judgment, and righteousness, in the earth: for in these things I delight, saith the LORD (Jeremiah 9:23-24).

Understanding and knowing Him should be foremost in our thoughts. Psalm 42:1-2 puts it, "As the hart panteth after the water brooks, so panteth my soul after Thee, O God. My soul thirsteth for God, for the living God." And David said in Psalm 63:1-2, "O God, Thou art my God; early will I seek Thee: my soul thirsteth for Thee, my flesh longeth for Thee in a dry and thirsty land, where no water is; To see Thy power and Thy glory."

A longing to know God isn't a fickle emotion that comes and goes with a soul-stirring song, a heart-wrenching sermon, or even the realization of a new Scriptural truth in our lives (though those experiences are valuable). It is a choice of the heart, not to be carried out in our own strength. Instead it requires a willingness to be taught, in whatever way He directs. His promise is sure. He will reveal Himself to us if that is truly our heart's desire. As Jeremiah went on to say in chapter 29:13-14, "And ye shall seek Me, and find Me, when ye shall search for Me with all your heart. And I will be found of you, saith the LORD." Oh, may we desire with all our heart that our Lord, who is our life, will reveal Himself to us!

> Therefore, if any man be in Christ, he is a new creature: old things are passed away; behold, all things are become new (II Corinthians 5:17).

With Christ's life imparted to us at the new birth, we become a "new creature," a new creation. Our new life isn't just the "old one" rehabilitated and spruced up with some religious education. It's totally different. Galatians 2:20 puts it so wonderfully: "I am crucified with Christ: nevertheless I live; *yet not I, but Christ liveth in me:* and the life which I now live in the flesh I live by the faith of the Son of God, who loved me, and gave Himself for me."

And with our new lives, the Lord not only wants us to know Him but also to yield ourselves to Him entirely. He is Master of our new life. As we come to know Him more fully and learn how worthy He is of our total trust and devotion, yielding to Him as Master becomes more and more natural. Yet there is always a struggle because it is always a choice. Still the victory is there for us through the power of our new life—Christ in us.

> Likewise reckon ye also yourselves to be dead indeed unto sin, but alive unto God through Jesus Christ our Lord. Let not sin therefore reign in your mortal body, that ye should obey it in the lusts thereof. Neither yield ye your members as instruments of unrighteousness unto sin: but *yield yourselves unto God, as those that are alive from the dead,* and your members as instruments of righteousness unto God (Romans 6:11-13).

Who reigns in our life? Is it the Lord; whose life it is? Or is it us giving in to sin in the weakness of our flesh? That question isn't answered just once; it's answered moment by moment in our lives. Little wonder we should "seek the LORD and His strength, seek His face continually" (I Chronicles 16:11).

When we let the Lord reign in our lives moment by moment, it is His strength that is sufficient. Ours can never be, but His always is.

How wonderful to know that we have the power of the Lord's resurrection life to claim against sin, and to give us victory and "life" in our lives. But how do we learn to live with the power and victory available to us? God has given us two extremely important "Guides" to our new life: His Holy Spirit and His Holy Word.

On the night that I was saved, the moment I trusted in the blood of the Lamb to take away my sins, God gave me the Comforter, the Holy Spirit, to come and dwell with me. If you know Jesus Christ as your personal Savior, you became the "temple" of the Holy Spirit also (I Corinthians 3:16). We were "born of the Spirit" (John 3:6) so that our spirits can now communicate with the Holy Spirit of God. And Christ promised that "when He, the Spirit of truth, is come, He will guide you into all truth" (John 16:13). We know that Jesus Himself is Truth (John 14:6) and that God's Word is truth (John 17:17). So we know that we can depend on the Holy Spirit to guide us as we seek to know our Savior and His Word.

> But the natural man receiveth not the things of the Spirit of God: for they are foolishness unto him: neither can he know them, because they are spiritually discerned. . . . But we have the mind of Christ (I Corinthians 2:14, 16).

I read the Bible when I was in the convent. I had my own opinion of it, but I did read it. There are lots of people that have opinions about Scripture. But you know what? There is no private or personal interpretation of it. We can't come up with a right interpretation on our own. The Bible's human writers "spake as they were moved by the Holy Ghost" (II Peter 1:20-

21). And it's only as the Holy Spirit gives us "spiritual discernment" that we can understand the truths of God's Word. Our puny brains can't comprehend the "things of the Spirit of God," but praise the Lord, because of the new life of Christ within us, "we have the mind of Christ!"

> Grace and peace be multiplied unto you through the knowledge of God, and of Jesus our Lord, According as *His divine power hath given unto us all things that pertain unto life and godliness,* through the knowledge of Him that hath called us to glory and virtue (II Peter 1:2-3).

Praise the Lord, He has given us all things for our new life with Him! Once we are saved, there isn't anything extra—like a "second blessing"—that we need. We just have to learn and then to enjoy experientially what we received from God the day we were redeemed.

We have the life of Christ within us and the Holy Spirit and God's Word to guide us. We've hardly scratched the surface of all that those truths can mean in our lives. But I pray that, as we look further at our "song" in other "seasons," the Holy Spirit will use God's Word to speak to your heart. And may you have a song of "new life" that shows forth His salvation from day to day.

New Life

New life in Christ! Abundant and free!
What glories shine, What joys are mine,
What wondrous blessings I see!
My past with its sin, The searching and strife,
Forever gone—There's a bright new dawn!
For in Christ I have found new life!

John W. Peterson
(1963) Singspiration

a Song for Spring

My Heart's Prayer

My new life I owe to Thee, Jesus Lamb of Calvary;
Sin was canceled on the tree, Jesus, blessed Jesus.

Humbly at Thy cross I'd stay, Jesus, keep me there, I pray;
Teach me more of Thee, each day, Jesus, blessed Jesus.

Grant me wisdom, grace and pow'r, Lord, I need Thee ev'ry hour.
Let my will be lost in Thine, Jesus, blessed Jesus.

Saviour, Thou hast heard my plea, Thou art near—so near to me;
Now I feel Thy strength'ning pow'r, Jesus, blessed Jesus.

H. P. Blanchard.
(1920) Ralph E. Stewart

selah time

1. How would you characterize "your life"—alive or dead? How would you characterize the life of Christ within you—alive or dead? Why?

2. Look again at Philippians 3:10. Knowing Christ means having an ongoing intimate relationship with Him. It is a relationship in which our understanding of Him and all of His wonderful characteristics is continually deepening. Are you seeking to know Christ?

3. We have looked at numerous Scripture passages in this chapter, and we will continue to do so as we proceed. Recognizing that "God's Word is truth" and that the Holy Spirit guides us "into all truth," will you ask God that He would indeed be your Guide as you consider His Word?

a Song for Summer

Summer is a time . . . of needful rain and of violent storms; . . . of warming sun and of severe droughts; . . . of growth.

~

Growth in our Christian life should be taking place from the time of our new birth until the time of our promotion to Glory. And as the growth of God's creation depends on rain and sunshine, we depend on the nourishment of God's Word (I Peter 2:2) and the instructive light of God's Holy Spirit.

While summer seasons hold many delights, they also hold the potential for devastating blows from droughts and storms. And for Christians, it's often those very difficult circumstances that bring us to a realization of the power of our God.

~

Chapter 3

A Song of Brokenness

Create in me a clean heart, O God; and renew a right spirit
within me. Cast me not away from Thy presence; and take not
Thy Holy Spirit from me. Restore unto me the joy of Thy salva-
tion; and uphold me with Thy free spirit. Then will I teach
transgressors Thy ways; and sinners shall be converted unto
Thee. Deliver me from bloodguiltiness, O God, Thou God of
*my salvation: and **my tongue shall sing** aloud of Thy right-*
eousness. O Lord, open thou my lips; and my mouth shall shew
forth Thy praise. For Thou desirest not sacrifice; else would I
give it: Thou delightest not in burnt offering. The sacrifices of
*God are **a broken spirit: a broken and a contrite heart,***
O God, Thou wilt not despise.

PSALM 51:10-17

As we're just beginning to consider some of the wonderful
truths concerning our new life in Christ, it may seem strange
that we take up the theme of brokenness. But this very theme
holds profound and precious nourishment for our souls. In a
real sense, it is in the depths of brokenness that the heights of
our divine relationship are found.

After I was saved, I spent seventeen years *trying* to live the
Christian life. Armed with an unusual testimony of salvation as
an ex-nun and several years of experience managing my life
with apparent success, I began speaking to ladies all over the
country. I gave them all kinds of helps for ordering their lives,
drawing themselves nearer to God, and avoiding the pitfalls of
sin. Much of what I was teaching was good advice, but some-

thing very important was missing in my life and, therefore, in my instruction.

> But to this man will I look, even to him that is poor and of a contrite spirit, and trembleth at My word (Isaiah 66:2b).

Mercifully, in the midst of all that activity, the Lord opened my eyes to what was happening in my own life. And He introduced me to the painful but life-changing process of brokenness. It was 1991. I had just launched Phebe Ministries to carry out my work with ladies, and I had set up my base in South St. Paul, Minnesota. Sensing something was amiss with a lady named Polly at my church there, I confronted her, expecting to expose her problem. Instead, I came face to face with mine.

She told me, "Wilma, you've been teaching ladies here and around this country to 'do, do, do.' Wilma, you're wrong! You have the cart before the horse. *It's not 'do, do, do'* that God wants from us—*it's to 'be'* right with Him. Then He will 'do' through us what He wants done!"

I was devastated. As she continued to explain, the Holy Spirit was impressing me with the horrible realization that she might be right and I might be wr...wro...wrong!

The moments, the hours, the days that followed were filled with tears and an excruciatingly painful search for answers. My pastor, Dr. Walter Olsen, confirmed Polly's assessment, and I ran to my Bible, pleading with the Lord for the truth from Him. He got my attention immediately with a look at the very lesson I was to teach that evening for the ladies' class in vacation Bible school. It was from John 15:1-5 about His being the vine and we the branches and the necessity of abiding in Him, because without Him we are unable to do anything.

When I had talked to Polly that day, she had used two particular passages of Scripture from Ezekiel 16 and Revelation 3. I don't remember everything that was said in connection with those passages. I do remember she talked about the first fourteen verses of Ezekiel 16 and how they describe all that God had done for Israel. Then, starting in verse 15, comes the description of Israel's wickedness despite God's goodness. It begins with, "But thou didst trust in thine own beauty."

The next morning as I was beginning my devotions, I was afraid to open my Bible. I sat in my chair, still in my night clothes, and talked with the Lord. I told Him, "God! I'm afraid to open my Bible. If I have been wrong all these years, I need to acknowledge my wrongs and make them right with You. I've sincerely taught all that I know about Your Word, but if I'm wrong, I need to know that. If this is just Polly's opinion, it doesn't matter. But if it's me that is wrong, then I want to know from You."

I took out an unmarked Bible, but I didn't know where to begin to look for the answers I needed. Then the thought came into my mind as if the Lord were speaking to me, "I know exactly where you are and what is happening today in your life. Just pick up where you left off yesterday in your Bible reading."

So I picked up the Bible reading schedule I was using . . . and my heart sank. The assigned reading for the day was Ezekiel 16—the very passage that Polly had talked to me about the day before. Fear struck my heart, and I started to cry. I knew right then that the Lord was telling me I had been wrong.

I read and reread Ezekiel 16 that day. Then the next morning in my devotions the Lord impressed on me to praise Him for what He was doing in my life. As hard and as humbling as this situation was, He prompted me to thank Him by praying through my favorite praising Psalms—Psalms 95 to 100.

> To day if ye will hear His voice, Harden not your heart, as in the provocation, and as in the day of temptation in the wilderness: When your fathers tempted Me, proved Me, and saw My work. Forty years long was I grieved with this generation, and said, It is a people that do err in their heart, and they have not known My ways: Unto whom I sware in My wrath that they should not enter into My rest (Psalm 95:7b-11).

When I read those verses, I knew the Lord had been wanting me to study them for several months, but I hadn't taken the time to do it. I set about to do it that morning, and was investigating the various words in the passage. When I came to the word "grieved" in Psalm 95:10, I somewhere came across the word "nauseate," even though that is not necessarily the meaning of "grieved" in that verse. Nevertheless, as soon as I saw that word "nauseate," my thoughts went immediately to Revelation 3:15-20. "I know thy works, that thou art neither cold nor hot: I would thou wert cold or hot. So then because thou art lukewarm, and neither cold nor hot, I will spew thee out of My mouth."

There I was, a fairly popular ladies' speaker. I felt I had the answers the ladies needed. I was content in what I was teaching. But could it be that my contentment with and pride in my own activity for God was making Him sick? Then I looked at verses 17 to 20.

> Because thou sayest, I am rich, and increased with goods, and have need of nothing; and knowest not that thou art wretched, and miserable, and poor, and blind, and naked: I counsel thee to buy of Me gold tried in the fire, that thou mayest be rich; and white raiment, that thou mayest be clothed, and that the shame of thy nakedness do not appear; and anoint thine eyes with eyesalve, that thou mayest see. As many as I love, I rebuke and chasten: be zealous therefore, and repent. Behold, I stand at the door, and knock: if any man hear My voice, and open the door, I will come in to him, and will sup with him, and he with Me (Revelation 3:17-20).

There I saw myself, wretched, and miserable, and poor, and blind, and naked. I saw how much I had been trusting in my own "spiritual abilities" to accomplish what I thought was God's work. My religious pride had blinded me to the real condition of my heart before the Lord. There He was knocking. What was I going to do?

Now I hadn't intentionally studied those passages in Ezekiel and Revelation just because God had used them with Polly. But when the Lord took me to both of those passages in my personal devotions to show me who I was and what I was doing, I realized at that point that I had nauseated the Lord by trying to live the Christian life my way instead of His way. He once again verified the point—"Yes, Wilma, this is you, and yes, you have been wrong!"

For the next month, I was afraid even to talk with people about the Bible. In fact, it seemed that the Lord emptied my mind of everything about Him and began to teach me anew. He showed me more Scripture passages to confirm my utter helplessness to do anything on my own. My discipline and formulas for Christian success crumbled at the revelation that these were merely attempts to please God on my own terms, through my own efforts, and in my own strength.

> Are ye so foolish? having begun in the Spirit, are ye now made perfect by the flesh? (Galatians 3:3).

At that point the Lord took me to this verse in Galatians, and the thought struck home. I was coming to the place where I was realizing that my miserable self-works couldn't please Him any more now than they could when I went to Him for the free gift of salvation. I was going to have to learn how to give up "my life," lived in the power of the flesh, and allow Him to live "His life" through me in the power of the Spirit.

There is much more about this truth concerning our weakness and God's strength and the necessity of allowing Him to work in and through us that I want to share with you. But permit me to come back to that in the next chapter. Right now I want to deal with the attitude of brokenness itself.

At that time, apart from my salvation, just about everything else concerning my life and ministry was in question. I had to re-examine what I was teaching ladies everywhere and let the Lord show me what was right. To find myself wrong about things was extremely humbling—and that was the point. God wanted to bring me to the realization that I needed to repent of my sinful pride and let Him have His way in my life.

> For thus saith the high and lofty One that inhabiteth eternity, whose name is Holy; I dwell in the high and holy place, with him also that is of a contrite and humble spirit, to revive the spirit of the humble, and to revive the heart of the contrite ones (Isaiah 57:15).

In my life the Lord used a confrontation with my religious pride to bring me to my knees in brokenness. The Scripture at the beginning of this chapter from Psalm 51 reminds us of King David. He was a man after God's own heart (I Samuel 13:14), but in his pride he tried to live life his way. He thought he could get away with adultery and murder, but, when Nathan, the prophet, pointed at him (II Samuel 12:7), he fell with a broken spirit before the Lord.

There are countless means the Lord may use to break our determination to depend on ourselves, living the Christian life in our own way rather than by His grace and strength. He may allow our pride to surface, as David's did, in a sin that humiliates us openly before others. He may take from us some particular object of our pride such as our physical strength, our career, a position of status, our dream house, or our future plans to show us how misplaced our values have been. Or perhaps He will allow other circumstances in our lives—health, family, or financial problems, difficult relationships, burdensome responsibilities, etc.—to bring to light in more subtle ways the disgusting pride we harbor within.

Do we know better than He about our families, our jobs, our health, our future? Are we demanding something from Him that He may not intend to give? Do we think that we have figured out how He must work in our lives and the lives of those around us without taking time to listen to His still small voice?

> Search me, O God, and know my heart: try me, and know my thoughts: And see if there be any wicked

way in me, and lead me in the way everlasting (Psalm 139:23-24).

So much of the emptiness and failure in Christian lives today stems from the fact that, often unconsciously, we are unwilling to let the Lord search our hearts and try our thoughts. He is always there, wanting us to open ourselves to the convicting power of the Holy Spirit, who can show us our self-willed and self-righteous attitudes and actions.

And the point is that we should want Him to search our hearts, not for His information because He certainly knows them already (Psalm 139:1-2), but so that He will open our eyes to our sin. Jeremiah 17:9-10a says, "The heart is deceitful above all things, and desperately wicked: who can know it? I the LORD search the heart, I try the reins [mind]." So often our own hearts and minds deceive us, hiding the sin that festers there. We need the light of God's Word, which is "quick, and power-ful, and sharper than any twoedged sword" and is a "discerner of the thoughts and intents of the heart" (Hebrews 4:12) to show us that sin so that we can repent in an attitude of broken-ness before Him.

We may be so busy "do-do-do-ing" the things we think He demands that we've closed off our hearts to the work He wants to do there. Right actions outwardly won't clean up our lives within. We must want His presence to rule our hearts. Then He can work His holiness out through us.

But we have to make the choice. Do we want that precious fellowship with Him that requires relinquishing control to Him? Are we really open to let Him convict us of the pride that causes Him pain? And when He does convict us, do we bow our heads in repentance or stiffen our necks in denial of sin?

> God resisteth the proud, but giveth grace unto the humble (James 4:6b).

Such openness with our Savior can demand a great price from us, because true repentance before God may involve actions visible to others. Are we willing to confess our sins, openly if necessary? And are we willing to make things right with others we have wronged?

I had to come to the place where I would admit that I was wrong and sorry, and that I needed to repent. I had travelled around America for years teaching ladies to "just do this, this, and this, and you will be fine. You will be content in your problems and your relationships." I was wrong. And I've had to admit it over and over again to ladies as I have returned to their areas in the country to speak to them at other meetings.

One of the tough things about brokenness is that it isn't something we face just once and "get it over with." It's a continuous process, an attitude of coming before the Lord moment by moment for His searching and trying and cleansing so that His life can be manifested fully in us. We must allow Him to break our wills. When we are tempted to reject His right to show us our sin, He reminds us that He "resists the proud but gives grace to the humble."

And why should we submit to an on-going encounter with brokenness in our lives? The answer lies so clearly in the example of our Lord who was willingly broken, not just in body but also in spirit, for us. We see Him kneeling in the garden praying, "Nevertheless not My will, but Thine, be done" (Luke 22:42). Such love demands that we let the mind of Him who humbled Himself and became obedient unto death be in us (Philippians 2:5-8).

So often we try to justify "natural human responses" to our circumstances rather than look at them, in truth, as sin. God doesn't want our excuses. He wants us to see ourselves and our sin—whether it be pride, bitterness, envy, wrong desires of any kind, self-pity, or whatever—as He sees us in truth. Then we are confessing the weakness of our flesh before Him and allowing Him to show us His strength by conforming us to His image. That's how His righteousness may be seen in us.

We allow Him to show us His forgiveness, His love, Himself. We are free then to delight in our God and enjoy that relationship of "new life" with Him—His presence and joy (Psalm 16:11).

a song of brokenness

It is in brokenness that we find the key to continuous revival in our lives. We agree to the fact that His ways are indeed best. Having it "our way" is not a concern, and what others think about us, right or wrong, is irrelevant if we are fully yielded to Him.

There is only One so just, so compassionate, so worthy to occupy the throne of my life or of yours and to rule there in complete wisdom. If brokenness dethrones me, or anyone or anything else that I may have placed on that throne, then I say, "Yes, Lord, break me! I desire to worship You and You alone, and 'my tongue shall sing aloud of Thy righteousness!'" (Psalm 51:14b).

HAVE THINE OWN WAY, LORD

Have Thine own way, Lord! Have Thine own way!
Thou art the Potter; I am the clay.
Mould me and make me After Thy will,
While I am waiting, Yielded and still.
Have Thine own way, Lord! Have Thine own way!
Search me and try me, Master, today!
Whiter than snow, Lord, Wash me just now,
As in Thy presence Humbly I bow.
Have Thine own way, Lord! Have Thine own way!
Wounded and weary, Help me, I pray!
Power—all power—Surely is Thine!
Touch me and heal me, Savior divine!
Have Thine own way, Lord! Have Thine own way!
Hold o'er my being Absolute sway!
Fill with Thy Spirit Till all shall see
Christ only, always, Living in me!

Adelaide A. Pollard
Copyright 1935. Renewal.
Hope Publishing Co., owner.

1. Have you ever experienced brokenness before the Lord in your walk as a Christian?

2. Right now are you willing to pray, "Search me, O God, and know my heart: try me, and know my thoughts: And see if there be any wicked way in me, and lead me in the way everlasting" (Psalm 139:23-24)? Is there something in your life right now that is the object of pride? Is it your Christian work, your position, a possession that is dear to your heart, your plans, or something else? Will you let the Lord break you and have His way in that matter?

Chapter 4

A Song of Deliverance

Thou art my hiding place; Thou shalt preserve me from trouble;
Thou shalt compass me about with songs of deliverance. Selah. I
will instruct thee and teach thee in the way which thou shalt go:
I will guide thee with Mine eye. Be ye not as the horse, or as the
mule, which have no understanding: whose mouth must be
held in with bit and bridle, lest they come near unto thee.

(PSALM 32:7-9)

The Lord is our salvation, delivering us from death to life, and He will be our deliverance in the storms of life. But throughout our new life there lurks an enemy from which we need continual deliverance in order to enjoy the sweet fellow-ship with our Savior. That enemy is our own tendency to live after the flesh with its selfish desires. Praise the Lord, we can find deliverance from "self" when He truly becomes our "hiding place" and we lose our "selves" in Him.

> Verily, verily, I say unto you, Except a corn of wheat fall into the ground and die, it abideth alone: but if it die, it bringeth forth much fruit. He that loveth his life shall lose it; and he that hateth his life in this world shall keep it unto life eternal (John 12:24-25).

John 12:24 is one of my favorite verses. Knowing that, a friend gave me a plaque with that verse on it several years ago. It's been a reminder to me ever since of an important truth, because that plaque didn't use all the words in the verse. It said, "Except a corn of wheat fall into the ground . . . , it abideth alone."

Did you notice? Something very important is missing. It should be, "Except a corn of wheat fall into the ground *and* die, it abideth alone." It has to die, and that's the key part of the verse. It has to die so that the new plant life can come forth from that old seed. And we have to die to our selves—our plans, our desires, our possessions, our old life in the flesh. Then that new life that is ours in Christ can spring forth into view. Christ can be seen in us.

We must die—let go of self and let Christ be our all in all. But so often we're afraid to die. Don't be afraid to die to your-self, because you will then have Him living in and through you unhindered. You will have peace and joy and contentment like you have never ever had if you will learn to die to yourself.

Death to self requires brokenness. Self-willed attitudes and actions cannot be extinguished while we still resist God's deal-ings in our life. An attitude of humility and repentance before the Lord, in a recognition of our own helplessness, is essential to this most desirable death. We must surrender our will to Him.

As we stand before the Lord, He demands "unconditional surrender." We cannot dictate the terms of that surrender—He does. But He is our loving Savior, not an enemy. He wants absolute surrender, not for our harm but for our greatest good. He knows that in us, that is in our flesh, "dwelleth no good thing" (Romans 7:18), and so He and all of His goodness must be in total control. He wants complete surrender to and dependence on Him. That is death to self.

> Not that we are sufficient of ourselves to think any thing as of ourselves; but our sufficiency is of God (II Corinthians 3:5).

Death to self is dependence on God, not ourselves. In gen-eral we tend to take pride in our independence—that is, in being able to accomplish things by ourselves. In so many ways we strive and strive for independence—for self-sufficiency in our lives. And the closer we come to it, the farther we get from the true source of our sufficiency. Our goal instead should be total *dependence* on our Lord in every part of our lives.

Self-reliance is a trait of the flesh that we are born with. Have you ever seen a child fight against holding a parent's hand while crossing a street or walking through a crowd? Or perhaps you've seen a child refuse help assembling a delicate toy, only to have it break in his hands. Such statements of independence, despite popular opinions, are not cute and amusing. The parent knows more about what's going on and has the child's safety and best interest in mind. For the child to reject the guiding hand is foolish and possibly dangerous.

As adults, we often grow frustrated with children and teens who refuse our wisdom but instead go and do something their own way, only to end up in trouble. Yet, we may go for days, weeks, or months at a time handling our lives in our own strength and in our own way, totally oblivious to Christ's life in us. Often even the "spiritual" things we do are done through self-discipline. We trust our own knowledge and abilities to teach that Sunday School class, encourage that friend, or even witness to that neighbor. An occasional distress may send us to the Lord begging for help. But, before we know it, we're right back in our old pattern of self-reliance again.

To die to self, however, is to become totally dependent on our Lord in everything, not independent. We must learn that without Him we can do nothing (John 15:5). Our lives left in His control are safe and will accomplish what He purposes.

From the beginning to the end of our days, we must recognize that it isn't us—our "selves"—who accomplishes anything in our lives. In our self-sufficiency we can only produce wood, hay, and stubble (I Corinthians 3:11-13). The Christ who lives within us must accomplish through us what He wants done.

Now, of course, that doesn't mean that we quit our jobs, stop paying our bills, ignore tasks like cooking and cleaning, and sit around reading and meditating on Scripture all the time. There are some who ridicule the idea of death to self and allowing Christ to live through us as if it would make us some sort of pious but mindless, irresponsible robots. However, allowing Christ to reign and live His life in and through us simply means that we let Him direct our thoughts and actions. Then we can draw upon His strength and resources to meet every responsibility and every need that He allows to come into our lives.

> That ye might walk worthy of the Lord unto all pleasing, being fruitful in every good work, and increasing in the knowledge of God; Strengthened with all might, according to His glorious power, unto all patience and longsuffering with joyfulness (Colossians 1:10-11).

Our Lord certainly does intend for us to "do" things. "For we are His workmanship, created in Christ Jesus unto good works, which God hath before ordained that we should walk in them" (Ephesians 2:10). He created us with our own unique personalities, talents, and opportunities in order to accomplish His purpose in our lives. However, He wants us never to forget that He is working in our lives to give us His energy, His perspective, His desire, and His determination. And when we are yielded to His inner working in our lives, He will do through us what He wants done. "For it is God which worketh in [us] both to will and to do of His good pleasure" (Philippians 2:13).

In the truest sense of the words, we shouldn't ask the Lord to "help us" do things. Yes, we rely on His help, but He is the One totally responsible for any accomplishment. We can't take any credit. Yet, when we ask Him to help us, we too often are trying to do things on our own. We're asking for just a "little bit" of His strength or provision to combine with ours for the situation. That attitude won't work. We don't need "portions" of help—we need Him. He doesn't give us the strength. He is the strength. We can't. He can. We must depend wholly on Him— and we must realize that in order to die to ourselves. Then, as we are sensitive and responsive to His leading in our lives, we can truly give Him the glory for what He does.

And He said to them all, If any man will come after Me, let him deny himself, and take up his cross daily, and follow Me.

For whosoever will save his life shall lose it: but whosoever will lose his life for My sake, the same shall save it (Luke 9:23-24).

We humans have such a strong inclination to hold on tight to our own interests. We cling to people, to possessions, to power, to prestige. But in Galatians 2:20 Paul pictured the Christian as "crucified with Christ" and Christ as alive in us. However, we so often fail to recognize that people on crosses can't hold on to anything.

Death to self requires letting go of those things that we can't "take with us." Of course that doesn't mean that we have to leave our families, homes, and jobs, take vows of poverty, and enter a convent or monastery to die to self. It does mean that we have to relinquish control of those things in our lives to the Lord.

I've learned to say a little phrase that has helped me to turn over the control of things in my life to the Lord. It's simply "It's okay!" "It's okay, Lord, that that person doesn't respond the way I want." "It's okay, Lord, if I can't buy that thing I think I need." "It's okay, Lord, that my plans for today must be cancelled." "It's okay, Lord, whatever that group thinks of me." "It's okay, Lord, that I can't control these circumstances in my life." "You, Lord, are in control of all these things. May Your will be done." When I consciously and willingly respond in such a way, I deny my "self," giving over my rights to God's control.

Notice that Luke 9:23 says that if we are to follow Christ, we must deny ourselves and take up our cross *daily*. Like brokenness, death to self is not a one-time act. It's an on-going choice on our part. But what a great reward becomes ours in the process, because when we lose our lives for His sake, we find that promised Christ-life in return.

> Knowing this, that our old man is crucified with Him, that the body of sin might be destroyed, that henceforth we should not serve sin. . . Likewise reckon ye also yourselves to be dead indeed unto sin, but alive unto God through Jesus Christ our Lord (Romans 6:6, 11).

Dying to self is dying to sin. When Christ died on the cross, He took away the penalty of our sin. But He also took away the power of sin in our lives. Our new birth made that death of sin's dominion in our lives a reality, but too often we don't live like it. We still have the choice of yielding ourselves to sin. We all know that just because we're saved, the temptations to sin do not go away. Too often we "serve sin" because we don't reckon or count ourselves dead to it.

But we do have the power, by right of the new life within us, to be dead to sin. We can say, "I don't have to act like this! I don't have to be like this! I choose to be different! I count myself dead, and I claim Christ's life and power in me!"

> If we say that we have no sin, we deceive ourselves, and the truth is not in us. If we confess our sins, He is faithful and just to forgive us our sins, and to cleanse us from all unrighteousness (I John 1:8-9).

The fact that we have the power to count ourselves dead to sin doesn't mean that we'll ever become sinlessly perfect in our walk this side of heaven. I John 1:9 is in the Bible because God knows we all have sin that we need to confess after we are saved. But when we do make the wrong choices—when we do yield ourselves to sin—there's no need to give up in guilt and despair. There is need to confess to God and receive His forgiveness for restored fellowship. And there is need to again reckon ourselves dead to sin. Death to self and sin is a continual yielding to Christ.

> For I know that in me (that is, in my flesh,) dwelleth no good thing: for to will is present with me; but how to perform that which is good I find not. For the good that I would I do not: but the evil which I would not, that I do. Now if I do that I would not, it is no more I that do it, but sin that dwelleth in me (Romans 7:17-20).

Until we get to the place where we recognize that there is nothing good in our flesh, we're not going to have victory over sin. When we sin, it's not just a slip or a mistake. It is dirty, rotten sin. In our strength there is nothing we can do to clean it up. We've got to understand that bad news before we can understand and accept the good news.

Before we were saved we were condemned by our sin. And then, when we were saved, we learned that we had to depend totally on the Lord for forgiveness and escape from the penalty of death and hell. Now as children of God, in the same way, we must depend totally on the Lord to find victory and power over sin in our lives. We must realize that we can do nothing. We cannot live the Christian life on our own. Remember how Romans 5:10 puts it: "For if, when we were enemies, we were reconciled to God by the death of His Son, much more, being reconciled, we shall be saved by His life."

So what can we do now? We know that it was His righteousness that was imputed to us [put on our account] at the time we were saved from the penalty of our sin (I Corinthians 1:30). But who can save us from this sinful flesh once we become a Christians? Paul goes on to ask and answer that question. "O wretched man that I am! Who shall deliver me from the body of this death? I thank God through Jesus Christ our Lord" (Romans 7:24-25a). Praise the Lord, *He is our deliverance!*

> Therefore, brethren, we are debtors, not to the flesh, to live after the flesh. For if ye live after the flesh, ye shall die: but if ye through the Spirit do mortify [put to death] the deeds of the body, ye shall live (Romans 8:12-13).

God's Holy Spirit does live in us, and by His power—not ours—we can habitually put to death the promptings of the flesh. Our flesh cannot control our thoughts and actions unless we give in to it. We must make the choice. By letting Christ reign in our hearts, we can then claim the power of God to tell our old flesh to "drop dead" when it tempts us to sin. We can rest assured that, "The Lord knoweth how to *deliver* the godly out of temptations" (II Peter 2:9a).

We've got to get to the place where we are willing to say, when the flesh rises up, "There it is, Jesus! It's showing up in my life. That's why You had to die on the cross." We can't change ourselves. All we can do is admit that we're wrong. We're letting the old flesh tell us what to do. But if we go to Jesus and confess it, our fellowship with Him will be sweet. And He will cleanse us from all unrighteousness—that is, from the power of sin in that area of our lives.

Death to self requires brokenness, surrender, and dependence. Humanly speaking, it's totally undesirable. But for those of us who know the Savior, it means life at its fullest. It means victory in Jesus.

We live in a world where everyone seems to be always "looking out for number one." Paul says in II Timothy 3:1-2 that in the last days "men shall be lovers of their own selves." But that should never be a description of those of us who know the Lord. When we know who He is and what He has done for us, our focus must not stay on ourselves. We must, with John the Baptist, say "He must increase, but I must decrease" (John 3:30).

> Because he hath set his love upon Me, therefore will I deliver him: I will set him on high, because he hath known My name. He shall call upon Me, and I will answer him: I will be with him in trouble; I will deliver him, and honour him. With long life will I satisfy him, and shew him My salvation (Psalm 91:14-16).

By continuously losing our life in Christ, our most precious "Hiding Place," we will increasingly find that He is everything our hearts could desire. "The things of earth will grow strangely dim in the light of His glory and grace!" As in His strength we die to self, He becomes our song of deliverance!

Not I, But Christ

Not I but Christ, be honored, loved, exalted;
Not I, but Christ, be seen, be known, be heard;
Not I, but Christ, in ev'ry look and action,
Not I, but Christ, in ev'ry tho't and word.

Not I but Christ, my ev'ry need supplying;
Not I, but Christ, my strength and health to be;
Christ, only Christ, for body, soul, and spirit;
Christ, only Christ, live then Thy life in me.

O to be saved from myself, dear Lord, O to be lost in Thee,
O that it might be no more I, but Christ, that lives in me.

A. B. Simpson

 *selah time*

1. Why does death to self require brokenness?

2. What are the ways that you strive for independence in your life? Analyze each one to see if it reveals a foolish self-reliance instead of dependence on the Lord.

3. Right now, what are the circumstances, people, or things that are causing concern in your life? Are you willing to give up trying to control each one and say "It's okay, Lord!"?

4. Are you trying to overcome sin in your own life through self-discipline? Why can't we gain the victory over sin that way?

Chapter 5

A SONG OF HOPE

*Blessed be the God and Father of our Lord Jesus Christ, which
according to His abundant mercy hath begotten us again
unto a lively [living] hope by the resurrection of Jesus Christ
from the dead.*

(I PETER 1:3)

We who know Christ as our Savior have a wondrous source
for our new life. It springs from the fact that Christ is in us.
Moment by moment we are becoming more and more like
Christ as we allow Him to live His life in and through us. Now,
we are never going to be totally like Jesus Christ until we see
Him face to face. What a thrill that will be! But until then, we
should constantly be willing to decrease to self—our old
flesh—thereby allowing His likeness to increase in our lives.
The Christlikeness *will* show—He will show Himself in a life
totally yielded to Him. *Christ in us,* that's "the *hope* of glory"
(Colossians 1:27).

> According to my earnest expectation and my hope,
> that in nothing I shall be ashamed, but that with all
> boldness, as always, so now also Christ shall be mag-
> nified in my body, whether it be by life, or by death.
> For to me to live is Christ, and to die is gain (Philippi-
> ans 1:20-21).

The Apostle Paul is speaking in these verses about Christ
being magnified, exalted, and praised through his present life
because he had Christ as his life here and now. Then, when he

died physically, he would experience in heaven all the wonders of Christ forevermore. What gain!

With Christ as our Savior we do have the certain hope of heaven when we die, but we don't have to wait for the "sweet by and by" to experience the joy of His presence (Psalm 16:11). We have "the Lord Jesus Christ, [who] is our hope" (I Timothy 1:1), and so as Christians we are never to be "Hopeless" in this life. Whatever the trials that we face (difficult circumstances, loneliness, lingering sinful habits, a discouragingly lifeless Christianity, or anything else you have in mind), we can find real and certain hope for right now in our Lord.

> Grace and peace be multiplied unto you through the knowledge of God, and of Jesus our Lord, According as His divine power hath given unto us all things that pertain unto life and godliness, through the knowledge of Him that hath called us to glory and virtue: Whereby are given unto us exceeding great and precious promises: that by these ye might be partakers of the divine nature, having escaped the corruption that is in the world through lust (II Peter 1:2-4).

Though I quoted verses 2 and 3 of this passage in Chapter 2 (A Song of New Life), I want to take a closer look at it now. Note how it speaks of grace and peace multiplying to you, growing in you, and abounding. Does that sound like your life? You certainly wouldn't be alone if you said "no."

All too often we Christians muddle along in our lives, yearning for grace [God's unmerited favor] and peace in our daily walk, but not knowing how to get them. Look at what these verses say. How do we get grace and peace in our lives? "Through the knowledge of God, and of Jesus our Lord!"

Then look at the next verse. See there that His divine power has given *us* "all things that pertain [are needful and suited for] godliness." We are equipped for godliness. He has already given us everything we need. And if you have ever been to one of my ladies' meetings, you know what "all" means—all means *all*, and that's all that all means! But look further. How do we appropriate [take for use] all of those things we so desperately need? "Through the knowledge of Him that hath called us to glory and virtue!"

We're back to that immeasurably important point that we touched on in Chapter 2. We need to know our God. We need to grow in our understanding of our Savior. We also need to increasingly comprehend the power and provisions He has placed so graciously at our disposal.

Now to explore all those riches is a lifetime occupation, and countless books have been and could be written about them. But right now I want to share with you a few thoughts that the Lord has used to touch my heart, to give me hope, and to increase His grace and peace in my life.

> Now unto *Him that is able* to keep you from falling, and to present you faultless before the presence of His glory with exceeding joy, To the only wise God our Saviour, be glory and majesty, dominion and power, both now and ever. Amen (Jude 24-25).

Now that's a wonderful thought! Our God is able! We are not able, but He is. And look at what He is able to do. He is able to keep us from falling. We stumble and fall constantly without His grace and power. We fall because of us—not Him (Hebrews 12:15). But when we claim His ability by faith instead of our own, we can "be strong in the Lord, and in the power of His might" (Ephesians 6:10).

> Now unto *Him that is able* to do exceeding abundantly above all that we ask or think, according to the power that worketh in us, Unto Him be glory in the church by Christ Jesus throughout all ages, world without end. Amen (Ephesians 3:20-21).

There it is again. He is able! He is able "to do exceeding abundantly above all that we ask or think." But how? According to the power that is already at work in us! We have His power,

45

but do we know it? Do we claim it? Do we allow Him to show Himself strong on our behalf, or do we go on *trying* to work out our problems, *trying* to deal with our difficulties, *trying* to do God's work without Him?

> And God is able to make all grace abound toward
> you: that ye always having all sufficiency in all things,
> may abound to every good work (II Corinthians 9:8).

Once more, *God* is able! And what is He able to do? "Make *all* grace abound toward you." (And you know what "all" means!) His grace is there for us, imputed to our account at salvation, and imparted to us as we by faith claim it. And we can claim it as we face every challenge in our lives. Our strength fails, but His grace is made perfect in our weakness (II Corinthians 12:9).

And what's more, because He is able to make all grace abound toward us, we have *all* sufficiency in *all* things! Remember, we are not sufficient of ourselves (II Corinthians 3:5), but through His grace we have all sufficiency in everything that He wants us to be or do. That's how we can "abound to every good work"—through His grace and His sufficiency.

> The eyes of your understanding being enlightened;
> that ye may know what is the *hope* of His calling, and
> what [is]the riches of the glory of His inheritance in
> the saints, And what is the exceeding greatness of *His*
> *power to us-ward* who believe, according to the work-
> ing of His mighty power (Ephesians 1:18-19).

Our labors for Him are not routines and obligatory acts carried out through self-discipline by our own will power. If they are, we can pat ourselves on the back for our accomplishments. But rather, they should be labors working out from hearts of love that are in tune with God, sensitive to His Word and His leading in our lives. Then, following His will, we can labor with His power and provisions, all the while giving Him the glory. This puts us in a position like that of the Apostle Paul when he said that he labored, "striving according to His working, which worketh in me mightily" (Colossians 1:29).

> Whosoever shall confess that Jesus is the Son of God, God dwelleth in him, and he in God. And we have known and believed the love that God hath to us. God is love; and he that dwelleth in love dwelleth in God, and God in him (I John 4:15-16).

Another thought that has been a great encouragement to me lately has to do with God's indwelling presence in my life. The Bible teaches that God is omnipresent—that He is everywhere at the same time (Psalm 139:7-10). That means that because I am a Christian, the triune God [Father, Son, and Holy Spirit] dwells not only in heaven, but IN ME as well! Let's take a look at some other Scriptures to further explain the reality of His presence in our lives.

Christ promised us the "Comforter" (Holy Spirit) to "abide with [us] forever" and said that He "dwelleth with [us], and shall be in [us]" (John 14:16-17). The Holy Spirit has a special ministry in our lives, comforting us, convicting us of sin, leading us into truth, and glorifying the Lord Jesus. I Corinthians 3:16 goes on to remind us that "ye are the temple of God, and that the Spirit of God dwelleth in you." And, we are "sealed with that Holy Spirit of promise, which is the earnest [down payment] of our inheritance" (Ephesians 1:13-14).

> I am crucified with Christ: nevertheless I live; yet not I, but Christ liveth in me. . . . (Galatians 2:20). . . . Christ in you, the hope of glory (Colossians 1:27)

Because the Holy Spirit dwells in me, Christ dwells in me as well. He's not just far away on a throne, focused on more important people and issues. Through the Spirit, He is in me, communing with me and caring for me every moment of every day. How wonderful are Christ's words while praying to the Father: "I in them, and Thou in Me" (John 17:23). And He also promised us, "I will not leave you comfortless: I will come to you" (John 14:18).

> Jesus answered and said unto him, If a man love Me,
> he will keep My words: and My Father will love him,
> and We will come unto him, and make Our abode
> with him (John 14:23).

How easy it is for us to look up toward heaven and won-der whether He's aware that we're down here. Does He really see from way up there the tough times we're going through? Well, He does, but He's never distant from us, never beyond our reach, never inattentive to the slightest detail of our lives. He's right here in us, knowing exactly what we're experiencing, and knowing every thought in our minds.

What a wonderful truth it is that God is in me, and that's really *hope*. I have no strength, but He has *all* strength. I can't see the future, but He knows the end from the beginning of everything in my life. I'm prone to fear, but He holds me safe (Deuteronomy 33:27). Nothing is going to surprise Him. I can place total confidence in Him and claim His strength, His com-fort, His love, His constant care, knowing that He is right here with me every second of every day. For I know that He "will never leave [me], nor forsake [me]" (Hebrews 13:5b).

> But ye are a chosen generation, a royal priesthood, an
> holy nation, a peculiar people; that ye should shew
> forth the praises of Him who hath called you out of
> darkness into His marvellous light (I Peter 2:9).

When Colossians 1:27b says "Christ in you, the hope of glory," that hope is sure for eternal glory in heaven. But it's just as sure for a victorious life, praising the Savior right now for His grace and power. Even in the storms and droughts of this life, He is our steadfast hope, able to do whatever it is that He wants done.

We don't have to set out to do something great for Him. We don't have to worry about being something great for Him. In the truest sense of the word, we don't have to *live for Him*. Instead, we need to *live Him:* to understand that *He is living in us,* and allow His life to show through us. His love will shine in our lives and His labors will be accomplished as He intends (Ephesians 2:10). He works in us so that He can work through us, because "it is God which worketh in [us] both to will and to do of His good pleasure" (Philippians 2:13).

> Now the God of hope fill you with all joy and peace
> in believing, that ye may abound in hope, through the
> power of the Holy Ghost (Romans 15:13).

What are the cares of your life right now? Have you felt hopeless because you are unable to deal with your difficult circumstances or because you are unable to have peace and joy in your Christian life? Our mighty God *is able* to give you hope. He, living in you, is your Hope.

MOMENT BY MOMENT

Dying with Jesus, by death reckoned mine;
Living with Jesus, a new life divine;
Looking to Jesus till glory doth shine,
Moment by moment, O Lord, I am Thine.

Never a trial that He is not there,
Never a burden that He doth not bear,
Never a sorrow that He doth not share,
Moment by moment, I'm under His care;

Moment by moment I'm kept in His love;
Moment by moment I've life from above;
Looking to Jesus till glory doth shine;
Moment by moment, O Lord, I am Thine.

D. W. Whittle

 *selah time*

1. Review the verses that tell us "God is able" (Jude 24; Ephesians 3:20; II Corinthians 9:8). How can you apply this truth to your life today?

2. Read the words to "Moment By Moment," the song above. Note the wonderful hope we have because God lives in us.

Chapter 6

A SONG OF TRUST

*He brought me up also out of an horrible pit, out of the miry
clay, and set my feet upon a rock, and established my goings.
And he hath put a new song in my mouth, even praise unto our
God: many shall see it, and fear, and shall trust in the LORD.*

(PSALM 40:2-3)

A song of joy may come easily in the brightness of day, but
often a song means even more when shadows surround us.
Discouragements, trials, griefs, frustrations, fears . . . whatever
the circumstances we face, Christ's song of grace and provision
is sufficient in the dark times as well as in the light. Psalm 42:8
says, "Yet the LORD will command His lovingkindness in the
daytime, and in the night *His song* shall be with me." Learning
to trust Him, who is so worthy of our trust, even in the darkest
nights of our lives, can put a song of praise in our hearts. It will
comfort us, and it will inspire trust in those who hear our song.

> Trust in the LORD with all thine heart; and lean not
> unto thine own understanding. In all thy ways
> acknowledge Him, and He shall direct thy paths
> (Proverbs 3:5-6).

Christ is our strength and our song in seasons of trouble
and hurt. Those are not simply words that we are to know in
our minds. They have got to move "sixteen inches" from the
mind into the heart (the inner part of our beings). Knowing in
your head what the Bible says can still leave you defeated and
depressed in your Christian life (just as people can know the

gospel in their heads but never accept it in their hearts). But knowing in your heart the truth of God's Word leads to trust and joy.

Psalm 119:11 says, "Thy word have I hid in *mine heart"*—not my head. It is good to memorize Scripture, but how does the Holy Spirit of God move a verse of Scripture from our heads to our hearts? What does He use? Quite often it's trials! In seasons of trouble and pain, He takes verses like Proverbs 3:5-6 from being just some words we remember to a truth that we experience first hand. In trials we cry out to the Lord and depend on Him to be true to His Word. And He never fails. When we do indeed trust in and acknowledge Him, He does direct our paths as He promised.

When a trouble comes and I say, "God! I don't understand!," I know that it is as if He is saying to me, "Wilma, I never told you that you have to understand. I told you to acknowledge Me as your God—I understand. I have a reason for what you are going through. Remember, Wilma, that I told you that I would never give you more than you could handle. Do you remember that all things work together for good (Romans 8:28)? Nowhere have I told you that all things feel good or are good, but that they work together for good to them that love God. Wilma, do you love Me? That's what's important. You are called according to My purpose—not yours. I'm not picking on you. I have a purpose for your good and for My glory!"

> We are troubled on every side, yet not distressed; we are perplexed, but not in despair; Persecuted, but not forsaken; cast down, but not destroyed; Always bearing about in the body the dying of the Lord Jesus, that the life also of Jesus might be made manifest in our body. For we which live are alway delivered unto death for Jesus' sake, that the life also of Jesus might be made manifest in our mortal flesh (II Corinthians 4:8-11).

The Apostle Paul could knowingly speak of being troubled, perplexed, and persecuted. All of us can identify with him at least some of the time, for none of us are trouble-free. For others of us, the trials we face seem constant and chronic. Whether they be health problems such as severe handicaps or disease, family problems like living with an unsaved spouse or handling a wayward child, dealing with major disappointments such as a crumbled career, or facing life single, divorced, or childless, there is cause to trust.

Look how Paul notes that in his trials he's not distressed, not in despair, and not destroyed. The reason is that he sees God's hand on him in the troubles, turning the pain experienced into great gain. For it was those very troubles that allowed the "life of Jesus" to show through the Apostle Paul. Therefore, he could trust the Lord and "take pleasure" in his weaknesses.

> And [the Lord] said unto me, "My grace is sufficient for thee: for My strength is made perfect in weakness." Most gladly therefore will I rather glory in my infirmities, that the power of Christ may rest upon me. Therefore I take pleasure in infirmities, in reproaches, in necessities, in persecutions, in distresses for Christ's sake: for when I am weak, then am I strong (II Corinthians 12:9-10).

It's in the troubling experiences of our lives, when our own strength is obviously insufficient, that we are most open to allowing Christ's strength to step in and become our sufficiency. And, having experienced His presence and power in our weakness, we give Him glory and grow in our trust and dependence—just exactly what He wants from us. Oh, that we might learn to trust in and depend on Him at all times, not just in those troubling times, because our strength can never be sufficient.

James 1:2 says, "My brethren, *count it all joy* when ye fall into divers temptations [or various trials]." And Paul, in the passage above, said *"Most gladly* therefore will I rather glory in my [trials]." How can we count it all joy and gladly glory in all the troubles we face? Because we know that God's grace is sufficient and because when we are weak, then we can be strong in the Lord.

But you know what? We don't like to be weak, because weakness makes us vulnerable, and we don't like to be vulnerable. We're afraid of pain—all kinds, both physical and emotional. We're afraid to say, "Lord, as You will, use the pains in my life to teach me of Your love, Your comfort, Your strength." We would rather that He simply eliminate all troubles from our lives. And yet, then, we would never know the depths of His grace.

How much better it is for us to yield to His molding, His bending, and His breaking. In our trials we can learn to depend on Him moment by moment for the strength that we need. And we can learn to count it all joy.

I have a dear friend with a severe physical disability, and it has meant a life of multiplied pains and hardships for her. She and I were talking one day with a new Christian, who was lamenting all of the troubles in her own life. The new Christian, with a note of bitterness in her voice, remarked, "Well, I guess I'll just have to grit through it!"

My friend, who had been through so many trials herself, responded, "No, you have to count it all joy!"

I thought to myself, if anyone else had said that, it would be easy to come back and say, "Yeah, right, easy for you to say!" But this friend of mine had learned to count it all joy through a lifetime of trials. Through countless pains and weaknesses, she has experienced the comforting strength of the Lord. She's learned to say, "It's okay, Lord!" and she's learned to trust Him to work things together for good.

A few years ago at a ladies' conference in Dayton, Ohio, I shared the thought that we should learn to say "It's okay"—give the situation over to the Lord—when we face troubles in our lives. A year later I was in the home of one of the ladies who had been at that conference. She said to me, "Wilma, remember you said that we have to learn to say 'It's okay!' during our trials?" She said, "I've said it hundreds of times since then, and do you know what? Every time I have said it, it's been okay!"

Letting Him have the control over the situations and circumstances of our lives is just what He wants us to do. "It's okay, Lord. I don't understand it. But You've promised me that Your grace is sufficient in it. Not *it was* or *it will be,* but *it is* right now, right smack dab in the middle of my trouble, Your grace is sufficient!"

> The LORD also will be a refuge for the oppressed, a refuge in times of trouble. And they that know Thy name will put their trust in Thee: for Thou, LORD, hast not forsaken them that seek Thee (Psalm 9:9-10).

Over and over again in Scripture the Lord reveals Himself to us, assuring us of His presence in our lives in just the ways we need Him. "God is our refuge and strength, a very present help in trouble," He proclaims in Psalm 46:1. In that same psalm, verse 10, He reminds us to "be still, and know that I am God."

When life's storms are raging, and when we are prone to shake with anxiety and fear, God tells us, "Be still! Know who I am! Understand My love for you and My care for you!" Psalm 9:10 says that we will put our trust in Him because we know His name.

And He has revealed Himself by name in many ways throughout Scripture. He is *Elohim,* God the Creator, who formed you and me in love for His glory, purpose, and pleasure. He is *El Shaddai,* the all-sufficient One who is all-powerful—the One able to nourish us, protect us, sustain us, and pour out His life in and through us. He is *Adonai,* our Lord and Master, and as such we must acknowledge Him. He is *Jehovah* (or *Yahweh*), the Self-Existent One, the eternal I AM. And to that name He adds so many revelations of Himself—*Jehovah-jireh,* "the LORD will provide," *Jehovah-shalom,* "the LORD is peace," *Jehovah-raah,* "the LORD my Shepherd," and numerous others.

God says that we will put our trust in Him when we know His name. Have we desired to know Him, to experience the truth of all He wants to reveal to us about Himself? How can we know Him as *El Shaddai* unless we allow Him to meet our needs, nourishing us and sustaining us in trials? It's in the turmoil and frustrations of our lives that we come to know Him as *Jehovah-shalom,* our Peace. In every difficulty, great or small, He is waiting to reveal Himself as everything we need. When we really know who God is, we will trust in Him—we will "roll" everything over onto Him—we will "cast all our care upon Him" for we will know (with our heads and our hearts) that He cares for us (I Peter 5:7).

> In every thing give thanks: for this is the will of God
> in Christ Jesus concerning you (I Thessalonians 5:18).

We can count it all joy and we can give thanks to the Lord, even for the hardest struggles of our lives, knowing that He is at work in our lives revealing Himself to us and through us. It is His will that we give thanks *in everything,* and to remain unthankful is to resist His will.

One time while I was speaking on this point to a women's group, a lady challenged me, saying "Yeah, you have to thank Him 'in' it, but you don't have to thank Him 'for' it!"

I replied, "Oh yes, you do!" Ephesians 5:20 says, "Giving thanks always *for all things* unto God." Thanking God, in and for all our heartaches, discouragements, failures, and needs, difficult though they may be, is exercising trust in Him.

> Be careful [anxious] for nothing; but in every thing
> by prayer and supplication with thanksgiving let
> your requests be made known unto God. And the
> peace of God, which passeth all understanding, shall
> keep your hearts and minds through Christ Jesus
> (Philippians 4:6-7).

Can we trust our God to be who He says He is and to do what He says He'll do? He says He is our peace, and He promises that His peace, which is beyond human understanding, *shall* keep our hearts and minds. If we don't trust Him, the result will be anxiety, troubled hearts and minds, and fears.

Sadly, many Christians become fearful in the face of troubles rather than trusting. But that's not God's intention for us.

Knowing Him and trusting Him will take away fears. II Timothy 1:7 says "For God hath not given us the spirit of fear; but of power, and of love, and of a sound mind." If we have anxious fear, we didn't get it from God!

> *Fear thou not;* for I am with thee: be not dismayed;
> for I am thy God: I will strengthen thee; yea, I will
> help thee; yea, I will uphold thee with the right hand
> of My righteousness (Isaiah 41:10).

It's certainly not God's desire that we have troubling fears. But how do we get over nagging fears like the fear of failure? How do we get over panic attacks or phobias like claustrophobia or aquaphobia? How do we get over any anxious fear?

If you have such fear, look at that fear and ask yourself, "Whom am I trusting? To whom am I turning to gain victory over that fear?" Undoubtedly the answer is "myself." If we try to handle fear ourselves, the result is always a fright. "I can't handle this!" "What am I going to do?" "I can't do it!" We run from circumstances and responsibilities to avoid having to deal with the fear. And in so doing, we make ourselves miserable and often frustrate the people around us.

An essential truth of the Christian life is that without Him, I can do nothing (John 15:5), but "I can do all things through Christ" because He is the One who gives me strength (Philippians 4:13). He is your strength. He is your very life. *You can't* get rid of your fears, but *He is able!* I John 4:18 says, "There is no fear in love; but perfect love casteth out fear: because fear hath torment. He that feareth is not made perfect in love."

Fear has torment. We know that's true, because we are certainly tormented when we have fear. So what does it mean that "perfect love casteth out fear?" It means that we need to go to the Lord and confess that we are lacking in His perfect love. That love is a characteristic of the fruit of the Spirit (Galatians 5:22), but if His Holy Spirit is not in control of our lives, we lack that love.

When anxious fears are oppressing our lives, we are trying to control circumstances and situations instead of letting God be in control. Instead of trusting Him, often unconsciously, we begin to blame Him for allowing the problems that are frightening us. That attitude causes our love for the Lord to dwindle and bitterness toward Him to grow.

When we recognize what we are doing, we must go to the Lord in brokenness, confessing our bitterness and lack of love for Him. We can then say to Him, "I choose to ask You to give me Your love. I know You love me, and I want You to create Your love in my life, flowing from me back to You (I John 4:19). I know You are allowing this trouble to try my faith and dependence upon You. It is for Your purpose. I choose to love You, to yield to Your will, and to allow *You* to control this circumstance."

"Nothing can get to me without Your permission. I can trust You. I want to bear all things that You allow in my life, believe all things, have hope in all things, and endure all things (I Corinthians 13:7). My love has failed, Lord, but Your love never fails. Please produce Your love in my life that will take away this fear." When we respond in such a way, denying our selfish desire for control, He will give us His love and cast out the fear.

Some time ago I went to a theme park with three friends. I pursuaded them to join me at one last attraction before we left the park. It involved riding a sort of train in which several cars were joined together. Two friends sat in the first car, and the other friend and I sat in the second. As the ride started, the train took us up through a dark and very close space. I didn't know until afterwards that both of my friends in the first car were troubled by claustrophobia.

When the ride was over, one of those friends came running toward me. She was so distraught that she wanted to wring my neck. She was really upset with me for getting her into that spot.

The other one, however, said to me, "Wilma, I just learned a great lesson in there! When I first got inside I was petrified, and inwardly I was screaming 'Let me out of here!' All of a sudden the only thing that kept coming into my mind was a verse you had quoted so many times: 'Thou wilt keep him in perfect peace, whose mind is stayed on Thee: because he trusteth in Thee' (Isaiah 26:3). I just kept saying that verse as well as any other verses I could think of at the time, and you know what happened? I calmed down inside. I don't remember anything that I heard or saw in there, but I did have the peace of God that passeth understanding, and it did keep my heart and mind through Christ Jesus!"

What a wonderful lesson to learn. Our torment will go away when we focus on the Lord. Trusting Him produces peace in our lives, regardless of the circumstances.

> Blessed be God, even the Father of our Lord Jesus Christ, the Father of mercies, and the God of all comfort; who comforteth us in all our tribulation, that we may be able to comfort them which are in any trouble, by the comfort wherewith we ourselves are comforted of God (II Corinthians 1:3-4).

In this world there is no escaping trouble. John 16:33 says, "These things I have spoken unto you, that in Me ye might have peace. In the world ye shall have tribulation: but be of good cheer; I have overcome the world." What a blessed comfort to know that *in Him* we can have peace (Ephesians 2:14).

May we turn to Him, yield to Him, love Him, and praise Him with a song of trust in our trials and in our fears. Through them all He will show us Himself so that we may know our wonderful God and Savior more fully. And by learning to trust Him as He works in our lives, we will gain a comfort and a faith that we can both treasure for ourselves and share with others.

'TIS SO SWEET TO TRUST IN JESUS

'Tis so sweet to trust in Jesus, Just to take Him at His word;
Just to rest upon His promise, Just to know, "Thus saith the Lord."

O how sweet to trust in Jesus, Just to trust His cleansing blood;
Just in simple faith to plunge me 'Neath the healing, cleansing flood!

A Song for Summer

Yes, 'tis sweet to trust in Jesus, Just from sin and self to cease;
Just from Jesus simply taking Life and rest, and joy and peace.

I'm so glad I learned to trust Him, Precious Jesus, Savior, friend;
And I know that He is with me, Will be with me to the end.

Jesus, Jesus, how I trust Him! How I've proved Him o'er and o'er!
Jesus, Jesus, precious Jesus! O for grace to trust Him more!

Words by Louisa M. R. Stead, c. 1882

selah time

1. Can you think of a trouble in your life that the Lord used to "move a passage of Scripture from your head to your heart"? How did God reveal Himself to you in that trial?

2. Is there something in your life that you haven't thanked God for?

3. Do you have any bitterness or lack of love toward the Lord because of any anxious fear (or any other circumstance) in your life?

a Song for Fall

Fall is a time . . . of urgent labor requiring endurance; . . . of harvest, of ingathering, of fruit; . . . of reflections on gratitude.

~

The fruitful seasons in our lives hold many rewards and encouragements as we see desires accomplished. But often, in those times, as needs press and labors multiply, we quickly forget the season's joys and blessings. Yet even then, Our Lord is waiting to remind us of His grace and provision.

Oh that we may experience the fruit of God's Holy Spirit at work in our lives. As He is the Vine and we the branches, may we allow Him to labor in and through us, because we know that we cannot bear fruit of ourselves (John 15:5). And may we always, throughout every harvest, have a heart filled with gratitude to Him who is the giver of all increase.

~

Chapter 7

A SONG OF PEACE

*To give knowledge of salvation unto His people by the remis-
sion of their sins, Through the tender mercy of our God;
whereby the Dayspring from on high hath visited us, To give
light to them that sit in darkness and in the shadow of death,
to guide our feet into **the way of peace**.*

(LUKE 1:77-79)

We live in a world full of turmoil. The evening news and the
morning paper are a constant witness to that fact. But not just
"the world" is full of turmoil—we often would say that "our
world" is full of turmoil. It's hard not to think of all the difficulties and perhaps the heartaches that we face at any given time.
And besides all the problems and hardships that assault us,
whether big or small, there are all those "people" who compli-
cate our lives.

Sometimes in stressful workplace environments, we have
to get along with the people we work with, we work for, or
who work for us. At home we have to deal with all the problems created or experienced by our family members—parents,
spouses, children, and other relatives. And of course we have to
try to keep a good relationship with friends and neighbors
regardless of those annoying things they sometimes do or say.

Then, on top of all those people, there is our church family. It surely would be wonderful if the Lord's love and life were
shining through everyone in the church body so that there
were never any interpersonal relationship problems with our
Christian brothers and sisters. But we aren't in heaven yet, and

so we can expect to experience a measure of discord even in church at times.

> Peace I leave with you, My peace I give unto you: not as the world giveth, give I unto you. Let not your heart be troubled, neither let it be afraid (John 14:27).

Sometimes the complications people add to our lives can make us wish that we could cloister ourselves away from all the strife. But let me assure you, becoming a nun is not the answer. True peace is not found in trying to escape from life's circumstances—it's found in Christ, and it's manifested in our lives as we "let the peace of God rule in [our] hearts" (Colossians 3:15).

Let's back up a little bit to find out why we may be lacking peace in our lives and relationships. First of all, what is peace? We might define it as harmony, serenity, or freedom from strife. Biblically, it includes the idea of completeness or wholeness. Regardless of the words we could use to describe it, we certainly know when we are and when we aren't experiencing it. In the first chapter of this book I told you about how I found peace with God through Jesus Christ when I was saved. Ephesians 2:13-14 speaks of that possession of peace by saying, "Now in Christ Jesus ye who sometimes were far off are made nigh by the blood of Christ. For *He is our peace* . . ."

In salvation Christ paid the penalty in full for our sins. The score was settled with God once for all so that our relationship with Him holds absolutely no condemnation (Romans 8:1). The result for us is an eternal relationship of peace with God. And because we have that peace in our new life with Him, it is only fitting that His *perfect peace* (Isaiah 26:3) should flow through us and be exhibited in our relationships with others.

> Abide in Me, and I in you. As the branch cannot bear fruit of itself, except it abide in the vine; no more can ye, except ye abide in Me (John 15:4).

Galatians 5:22-23 tells us that peace is a characteristic of the fruit of the Spirit, just like love, joy, longsuffering, and the others. Therefore, the "peace of God" is something the Holy Spirit produces in our lives as we abide in Christ, our True Vine. If we're not experiencing peace in our relationships, then something's wrong with our connection to the Vine.

Remember, we can't live the Christian life in our own strength after we are saved. We are totally dependent on the new life of Christ within us. In John 15:5, you will recall, the Lord tells us, "I am the Vine, ye are the branches: He that abideth in Me, and I in him, the same bringeth forth much fruit: for *without Me ye can do nothing."* Christ is the Vine and we are the branches. The branches do not produce the fruit of the Spirit—they simply hold the fruit.

It is the "sap'" which produces the fruit on a natural tree. The Holy Spirit, with all due respect to the holiness of God, is the "Sap" of God. He produces His fruit in us if we will keep the channel clean. But You and I can quench the Spirit of God in our lives with sin (I Thessalonians 5:19). When we harbor sin in our lives, we clog up the channel and break our nourishing connection with the Vine. And a sin which often hinders the flow of peace in our lives is bitterness.

> Looking diligently lest any man fail of the grace of God; lest any root of bitterness springing up trouble you, and thereby many be defiled (Hebrews 12:15).

Ephesians 4:26 says, "Be ye angry, and sin not: let not the sun go down upon your wrath." As a pastor in Colorado spoke on the life of Joseph, he quoted this verse and asked, "When you go to bed angry, how do you wake up?" From the second row I responded, "angry!" He looked right at me, called me by name, and said, "No, Wilma. You'd wake up bitter." I knew immediately what he meant.

Anger may or may not be sin in our lives. God displays anger toward sin and evildoers, and there are certainly circumstances when we also can have such "righteous" anger. But all too often our anger is anything but righteous. It may spring from disappointment, jealousy, irritation, hurt feelings, abuse, or any number of causes, real or imagined.

Anger is hurtful enough when we display it in short outbursts that we soon forget. However, by nursing grudges we quickly turn our anger into bitterness. And the bitterness which may have stemmed from one incident doesn't only pour out of us toward the particular person or group involved. It begins to affect all of our relationships.

When we are bitter, we are easily irritated with people. We become sharp and disagreeable toward them. It's virtually impossible to display a sweet disposition when we are bitter, and it often shows on our faces with a big old "poochie lip."

> But if ye have *bitter envying and strife* in your hearts, glory not, and lie not against the truth. This wisdom descendeth not from above, but is earthly, sensual, devilish. For where envying and strife is, there is confusion and every evil work. But the wisdom that is from above is first pure, then *peaceable,* gentle, and easy to be intreated, full of mercy and good fruits, without partiality, and without hypocrisy. And the fruit of righteousness is sown in *peace* of them that make *peace* (James 3:14-18).

Our deceitful hearts (Jeremiah 17:9) often try to hide the true nature of our attitudes toward others. We try to excuse our ill feelings as being deserved by those we believe have wronged us. After all, it will serve them right if we snub them a bit. And besides, we don't need a close relationship with them anyway.

Wait a minute! When I am irritated because someone "did me dirty," God wants me to see that it was not the thing that the person did to me that matters—it's my reaction to it! Proverbs 13:10 says, "Only by pride cometh contention," and that contention [strife] takes root in my life because of pride, regardless of the other person's role in the matter.

a song of peace

The letter "I" is the center of "pride" and the center of "sin." "I" is that old fleshly self. Instead of being dead to self and sin, "I" want to feel sorry for myself. "I" want vengeance.

> Recompense to no man evil for evil. Provide things honest in the sight of all men. If it be possible, as much as lieth in you, live peaceably with all men. Dearly beloved, avenge not yourselves, but rather give place unto wrath: for it is written, Vengeance is Mine; I will repay, saith the Lord. . . . Be not overcome of evil, but overcome evil with good (Romans 12:17-19, 21).

Perhaps you're saying right now that to react peaceably is well and good when the hurt is something minor, but you have been hurt in a serious way. You may know the horror of rape or sexual or physical abuse. You may have a spouse who has cheated on you. You may have been swindled out of your savings. You may have been falsely and spitefully accused of some misdeed. You may have been betrayed by a Christian leader that you once respected.

No one could take these and other such circumstances lightly. The sins involved are heinous, but the fact remains that the people involved have to answer to God for what they did. And you have to answer to Him for your responses. Humanly speaking, a reaction of bitterness and even hatred is natural. But it is also a fleshly response that *enslaves you* to continuous frustration and misery in your life. It affects you physically, emotionally, and spiritually (Psalm 38:1-18), and it makes you act foolishly (Galatians 5:16-21a). You'll never know peace as long as you hang on to the bitterness.

> And grieve not the Holy Spirit of God, whereby ye are sealed unto the day of redemption. Let all bitterness, and wrath, and anger, and clamour, and evil speaking, be put away from you, with all malice: And be ye kind one to another, tenderhearted, forgiving one another, even as God for Christ's sake hath forgiven you (Ephesians 4:30-32).

But how can we get rid of bitterness, especially when the wounds are very deep? We can't, but our Lord can. However, He leaves the choice up to us. Will we allow Him to point out the pride and bitterness in our lives? Will we react in brokenness and let Him have His way with us?

By confessing our bitterness to Him and expressing our desire that He remove it from us, we allow Him to open the channel and release the flow of the Holy Spirit's life-changing "sap" through us. We can experience His love toward those who have wronged us. We can have His longsuffering [patience] toward them and know His peace as we deal with them, regardless of their reaction to us.

> For if ye forgive men their trespasses, your heavenly Father will also forgive you: But if ye forgive not men their trespasses, neither will your Father forgive your trespasses (Matthew 6:14-15).

A necessary ingredient in dealing with bitterness is coming to the place of forgiveness. Christ gave us a strong motive for forgiving those who have wronged us. If we won't forgive, God won't forgive us either. We need His forgiveness to restore sweet fellowship with Him (I John 1:9), and we must also seek His grace that will enable us to forgive our offender.

It doesn't matter if the wrongs against us are "big" or "little," few or many. Remember that the Lord also told Peter that he should forgive a brother's sin against him not just seven times, but "seventy times seven" (Matthew 18:21-22). How's your math? That's 490 times! Forgiveness is necessary regardless of the wrong or wrongs done to us if our relationship with the Lord is to be kept right. When our heart is right with Him, we can have peace in our lives.

Christ was our perfect example in forgiving those who wronged Him. According to I Peter 2:23, "When He was reviled, [He] reviled not again; when He suffered, He threatened not; but committed Himself to Him that judgeth righteously." Our response to wrongs needs to be the same. We must commit

ourselves or entrust ourselves to God in the assurance that He
will deal justly with everyone involved.

> And Joseph called the name of the firstborn Manasseh:
> For God, said he, hath made me forget all my toil, and
> all my father's house. And the name of the second
> called he Ephraim: For God hath caused me to be fruit-
> ful in the land of my affliction (Genesis 41:51-52).

In the book of Genesis we read of how Joseph was treated by
his own brothers. Some wanted to kill him, but they settled on sell-
ing him into slavery instead. And if that wasn't enough to get bitter
about, Joseph was falsely accused, put into prison, and even forgotten by one he had helped while there. But he did not pine
away in self-pity. His trust in God remained firm through the
reproaches and persecutions. Not only did he find grace to forgive—he also found grace to forget (Genesis 41:51; Hebrews 4:16).

Like Joseph, we must find God's grace to enable us to forget the wrongs we've suffered and to show God's love to the
people who committed them. I'm not saying that we won't
remember what they've done at all, but rather that we won't
remember them in bitterness. Thoughts of them won't stir up
the poisons of anger and strife, thereby robbing us of peace.

Look what God did for Joseph as he was willing to forget
the wrongs against him. God made him "fruitful . . . in the land
of [his] affliction." God didn't have to take him out of the place
of affliction to bless him. He blessed him right smack dab in
the middle of it. And that's exactly what the Lord will do for us,
too, if we're trusting Him to deal with our problems.

> (For the weapons of our warfare are not carnal [of the
> flesh], but mighty through God to the pulling down
> of strong holds;) Casting down imaginations [argu-
> ments], and every high thing that exalteth itself
> against the knowledge of God, and bringing into cap-
> tivity every thought to the obedience of Christ
> (II Corinthians 10:4-5).

Our thoughts about injustices can easily lead to bitterness, and fleshly weapons can't gain the victory. We're in a battle, but it's not our battle. Satan wants to keep a stronghold of bitterness in our minds. But through Christ we can capture our thoughts, keeping them Christlike rather than carnal.

The Holy Spirit is in us every moment. He's constantly saying, "What are you thinking?" Proverbs 23:7 says that as a person "thinketh in his heart, so is he." We are responsible for our thoughts, and they indicate what kind of person we are. When wrong thoughts come and the Holy Spirit convicts, do we disregard His prompting and continue to think on them? Or are we willing to bring those thoughts into captivity and obedience?

The thoughts of difficult situations that discourage us and thoughts of people who cause us pain will come back, but we choose whether we are going to retain them or not. We must make the choice. And the right choice is to refuse to think the wrong thoughts. We can pray, "Lord, You told me what I am supposed to be thinking on: things that are true, honest, just, pure, lovely, of good report (Philippians 4:8). I choose to think on those things. Focus my attention on You, on Your Word, and on other things that please You."

And the peace of God, which passeth all understanding, shall keep your hearts and minds through Christ Jesus. Finally, brethren, whatsoever things are true, whatsoever things are honest, whatsoever things are just, whatsoever things are pure, whatsoever things are lovely, whatsoever things are of good report; if there be any virtue, and if there be any praise, think on these things. Those things, which ye have both learned, and received, and heard, and seen in me, do: and the God of peace shall be with you (Philippians 4:7-9).

Forgiveness is a choice—an act of the will. No matter how strong our inclination to bitterness may be, we can still ask God to forgive the person through us, and He will. The choice then is to be "bitter" or "better." What is the difference between those two words? The letter "I." With the "I" we focus on ourselves instead of on God and others, and the selfish thoughts make us bitter. But God wants to make us better. What is your choice?

So what will all this mean in our relationships? When Christ works in us and lives through us, we can display a "supernatural" love and forgiveness in our lives just as He did for us. It will be a forgiveness that refuses to dredge up bitter memories. And it will be a love that continually seeks peace with each person that touches our lives (Psalm 34:14).

> And Joseph said unto them, Fear not: for am I in the place of God? But as for you, ye thought evil against me; but God meant it unto good, to bring to pass, as it is this day, to save much people alive (Genesis 50:19-20).

There are some further lessons we can learn from Joseph's example. In Genesis 45:5 he told his brothers, "Now therefore be not grieved, nor angry with yourselves, that ye sold me hither: for God did send me before you to preserve life." Joseph learned to see his brothers as God's agents. They had acted wrongly, but God's purposes were at work in Joseph's life. Much good was accomplished because of what happened. And Joseph didn't seek revenge as he certainly could have if he had responded according to the flesh. He simply let the Lord work out the situation through him in a gracious and loving way. What a tremendous testimony he has, and what a wonderful model he is for us!

Looking back at Joseph's situation, we can see so very clearly how "all things work together for good to them that love God" (Romans 8:28). In our own lives, without the overall perspective that we have on Joseph's life, it's hard to rest in the assurance that God's purposes are at work in our lives also. Nevertheless, even those trying relationships that we face are a part of His plan to break us, to mold us, and to make us a vessel for displaying His perfect peace.

A Song for Fall

LIKE A RIVER GLORIOUS

Like a river glorious Is God's perfect peace,
Over all victorious In its bright increase;
Perfect, yet it floweth Fuller every day,
Perfect, yet it groweth Deeper all the way.

Hidden in the hollow Of His blessed hand,
Never foe can follow, Never traitor stand;
Not a surge of worry, Not a shade of care,
Not a blast of hurry Touch the Spirit there.

Every joy or trial Falleth from above,
Traced upon our dial By the Sun of Love.
We may trust Him fully All for us to do;
They who trust Him wholly Find Him wholly true.

Stayed upon Jehovah, Hearts are fully blest;
Finding as He promised, Perfect peace and rest.

Frances R. Havergal

1. Is there someone in your home, church family, or work-place whom you have allowed to rob you of your peace?

2. Have you suffered a serious wrong from someone, and are the thoughts of that wrong making you bitter?

3. How do your responses to wrongs compare with the responses of Jesus and Joseph?

4. With Proverbs 23:7 in mind ("For as he thinketh in his heart, so is he"), what kind of person would your thoughts indicate that you are?

Chapter 8

A SONG OF LOVE

The LORD thy God in the midst of thee is mighty; He will save,
He will rejoice over thee with joy; He will rest in His love, He
will joy over thee with singing.

(ZEPHANIAH 3:17)

Many of us have known and sung the song "Jesus Loves Me" from the time we were knee-high. It's a wonderful song expressing a wonderful truth, a truth that is the very heart of our Christianity. Yet, with all its simplicity, do we really understand what it means in our lives that Jesus loves me? Put your name in the song in place of the "me." Do you know the breadth and length and depth and height of Christ's love for you?

> That Christ may dwell in your hearts by faith; that ye, being rooted and grounded in love, May be able to comprehend with all saints what is the breadth, and length, and depth, and height; And to know the love of Christ, which passeth knowledge, that ye might be filled with all the fullness of God (Ephesians 3:17-19).

These verses are part of a prayer that the Apostle Paul expresses for the Ephesian Christians, a prayer that we can and should pray for ourselves and for one another. And as Paul continues in verse 20, he sets forth perhaps the greatest encouragement of all to us. He says, "Now unto *Him that is able* to do exceeding abundantly above all that we ask or think, according to the power that worketh in us." Isn't it wonderful that God is able to make His love real to us today in our daily walk here on earth?

77

Jesus' love for us passes human knowledge. We just can't grasp it on our own, even by studying Bible doctrines, or by reading good Christian books, or even by reading the Bible for hours at a time. Those things are certainly good and are used by the Lord as the means by which He instructs us. But ultimately it is God's Holy Spirit at work in us that reveals Christ and His amazing love to us. In II Thessalonians 3:5 Paul prayed for "the Lord [to] direct your hearts into the love of God." When we want to know and experience His love more fully, He delights in revealing that love to us in very personal ways.

> Charity [love] suffereth long, and is kind; charity [love] envieth not; charity [love] vaunteth not itself, is not puffed up [arrogant], Doth not behave itself unseemly [rudely], seeketh not her own, is not easily provoked, thinketh no evil; Rejoiceth not in iniquity, but rejoiceth in the truth; Beareth all things, believeth all things, hopeth all things, endureth all things. Charity [love] never faileth . . . . (I Corinthians 13:4-8a).

I Corinthians 13 is often called the "love chapter" because love is indeed its theme. It has served as a text for many fine devotionals, sermons, and books. Perhaps you've seen or heard I John 4:8 and 16 used in connection with the verses above. Both of the verses in I John clearly state God is love. Therefore, we can substitute "God" for "charity" (which is love) in the passage above. In other words, *"God* suffereth long, and is kind; God envieth not;" etc.

Do you see what the love chapter actually reveals about God's love for us? Think for a moment about the qualities you would want in a close friend, a confidant, someone to whom you could bare your soul. Can you imagine finding a friend who perfectly displayed all of the qualities brought out in I Corinthians 13? Wouldn't you long for a close relationship with such a friend, a friend who loved you perfectly? You have that kind of Friend in Jesus!

Let's look closer at the love our Savior has for us. First we must recognize that He proved the supreme degree of His love by making the greatest, most needful sacrifice for us. "For God *so loved* the world, that He gave His only begotten Son . . . ." (John 3:16). We were helpless and hopeless on our own, but God Himself looked down in love, became flesh, and in total humility shed His own blood to redeem us.

> But God, who is rich in mercy, for His *great love* wherewith He loved us, *Even when we were dead in sins,* hath quickened us [made us alive] together with Christ . . . And hath raised us up together, and made us sit together in heavenly places in Christ Jesus (Ephesians 2:4-6).

And look, He demonstrated His wondrous love while we were still wallowing in our sins. "But God commendeth [demonstrated] His love toward us, in that, while we were yet sinners, Christ died for us" (Romans 5:8). Even then He sought us, not only, to be our Savior and Lord, but also to be our Friend. For in John 15:13 He says, "Greater love hath no man than this, that a man lay down his life for his friends."

I Corinthians 13:5 depicts love as being unselfish, not self-seeking. What greater act of selflessness could our Lord have done than to give His very life for wretched sinners like us? How blessed it is for you and me to truly realize that Christ "loved me [each of us individually] and gave Himself for me" (Galatians 2:20).

> According as He hath chosen us in Him before the foundation of the world, that we should be holy and without blame before Him in love (Ephesians 1:4).

We Christians, of course, have come to realize that Jesus loved us enough to die and pay the penalty for our sin. But somehow, many of us get the feeling that His love has to be earned after salvation by good behavior. Let me ask you a question. How many of our sins did Jesus pay for? All of them! I John

1:7 says that "the blood of Jesus Christ His Son cleanseth us from all sin." And you know what "all" means. It certainly doesn't mean just those sins we committed before we were saved.

In the first chapter of this book we talked about how we are "justified" when we are saved, made to be "just as if we'd never sinned." When God looks on us through the blood of Christ, he sees us pure and sinless now and forever. As Ephesians 1:4 so beautifully puts it, we are "holy and without blame before Him in love." And Romans 8:1 states confidently, "There is therefore now no condemnation to them which are in Christ Jesus."

> And you, that were sometime alienated and enemies in your mind by wicked works, yet now hath He reconciled In the body of His flesh through death, to present you holy and unblamable and unreprovable in His sight (Colossians 1:21-22).

Now am I saying that once we are saved, because God sees no sin in us, we should feel free to sin? Certainly not! But let me cover that point in the next chapter. Right now it is extremely important that we understand that God's love for us is not conditional. Our behavior does not affect God's love for us. When we as Christians have sin that besets us, it does not make God withdraw His love and turn away from us in disgust.

So many Christians today . . . and maybe you are one of them . . . look at themselves as failures. They can't seem to get the victory over sin in their lives. They can't seem to live with joy and blessing like some "perfect" Christian they know. They think God is watching in anger as they miserably stumble through life.

Look back at I Corinthians 13 again. Note that God's love "suffereth long." He's never impatient with us. He knows our frame. He remembers that we are dust (Psalm 103:14). He is endlessly compassionate with us. See, too, that God's love is "not easily provoked" and thinks "no evil."

a song of love

God in love sent His Son "that we might live through Him" (I John 4:9). But when we fail to let Christ's life in us gain the victory and instead let our selfish pride turn us to sin, God is not erupting in rage and calling us names (like some humans we may know). His compassion doesn't fail us. His love is ever constant, ever sure.

> Who shall separate us from the love of Christ? shall tribulation, or distress, or persecution, or famine, or nakedness, or peril, or sword? . . . . Nay, in all these things we are more than conquerors through Him that loved us. For I am persuaded, that neither death, nor life, nor angels, nor principalities, nor powers, nor things present, nor things to come, Nor height, nor depth, nor any other creature, shall be able to separate us from the love of God, which is in Christ Jesus our Lord (Romans 8:35-39).

The Lord who loved us and died to save us doesn't turn around in disappointment afterward and tell us to "get lost" because we can't measure up to His standard. Far from it! He tells us in the above verses that there isn't anything that "shall be able to separate us" from His love. In I Corinthians 13 we learn that His love *never fails*. It goes on and on to bear and believe and hope and endure *all things*. What wondrous love!

We can't determine whether or not God loves and accepts us by our fickle feelings. We must instead look to the truth of Scripture where He constantly assures us of His ongoing love: "Yea, I have loved thee with an everlasting love: therefore with lovingkindness have I drawn thee" (Jeremiah 31:3).

If Christ is indeed your Savior, know most assuredly that He loves you. He accepts you. You are precious in His sight. If you are doubting His love for you, just ask Him to use His Word to comfort your heart and give you that blessed assurance.

> Thus saith the LORD, Let not the wise man glory in his wisdom, neither let the mighty man glory in his might, let not the rich man glory in his riches: But let

him that glorieth glory in this, that he understandeth and knoweth Me, that I am the LORD which exercise lovingkindness, judgment [justice], and righteousness, in the earth: for in these things I delight, saith the LORD (Jeremiah 9:23-24).

This old world tells us that we have to get our identity, our "self-image," from what we do. Therefore, we can have self-esteem or feel good about ourselves if we do good, important, and worthwhile things. In that reasoning, people can glory in being professionals (teachers, doctors, real estate agents, etc.), in doing what they do as a career. They can glory in the talents or characteristics they display (as musicians, artists, athletes, gourmet cooks, or having a good figure or great strength, etc.). They can glory in what they've acquired (money and other possessions). Or they can glory in the responsibilities they fulfill and in the people who need or respect them (parenting, church work, civic duties, children, friends, etc.).

But God clearly tells us that we can't glory in any of those things. Either they will puff us up in pride (as we try to take the credit for God-given talents, possessions, opportunities, etc.), or they will fail us. We can lose jobs and money, and we certainly can lose our figures. People may not appreciate our talents. And regardless of our self-discipline, we still blow it at times when it comes to our responsibilities and relationships. To disregard God's direction and try to find our self-worth in such things is downright foolish.

What's more, when we try to find our identity in what we do, sinful behavior becomes a part of that identity. What I mean is that when we as Christians allow sin to beset us, we think of that sin as a part of who we are, and thus we have to take the label of the sin. We tie our weaknesses to our self-concept, seeing ourselves as hotheads, complainers, liars, cheaters, drunkards, adulterers, homosexuals, etc. We think of ourselves as rotten, sinful worms. We sink into despair and defeat because, in our flesh, we think that God couldn't love us as we are.

Hey, wait a minute! *Nothing* can separate us from the love of God! Who wants us to think that God stops loving us when we fall into sin? It's certainly not God! He has repeatedly assured us of His constant love. But Satan, that old deceiver, surely does delight in getting our focus away from our true relationship with the Lord and onto ourselves instead. We play right into the devil's hands when we think our identity comes from all those things we do or have. Satan knows that we're looking for victory and acceptance in all the wrong places, and he wants to keep us in the dark.

No! We who know Christ as our Savior cannot take our cues from the god of this world. We must refuse to both glory in or despair in the things we do. Instead, we must find our true identity in *who we are* before God. John 8:32 says that you "shall know the truth, and the truth shall make you free." Knowing who we truly are will set us free from the false expectations and condemnations that we may have placed upon ourselves. It can even set us free from the false expectations and condemnations that other people, even religious leaders or groups, may have placed upon us.

So, who am I as a Christian? If we will but look at the truth of Scripture to find out, we need not be defeated. We will see that God has given us the victory already.

> Therefore if any man be *in Christ,* he is a new creature: old things are passed away; behold, all things are become new (II Corinthians 5:17).

Yes, before we were saved we were wretched, sinful worms. We were incapable of pleasing God. We were headed for death and judgment because of our sin. But now we have that *new life* we talked about in chapter two. We are blood-washed, clean, and pure before God. He doesn't look at us and see that "old man" any more with its stains of sin. He looks at us and sees the life of Christ within us. We are truly justified in His sight. We are dead, our lives are hid with Christ in God, and Christ Himself is our life (Colossians 3:3-4). Therefore, the Father sees not us, but us in Him. Praise His Name!

A Song for Fall

From the moment that we were reconciled to God by the death of His Son (Romans 5:10), we are forever identified with Christ. We are positionally "in Christ." We no longer have to claim our sin, the sin that He died and paid for, because we are made "the righteousness of God *in Him*" (II Corinthians 5:21). We claim His righteousness, not our own. We are born again as a "new creature," with the life of Christ becoming our very life. "For as in Adam all die, even so *in Christ* shall all be made alive" (I Corinthians 15:22).

Being in Christ affords us *everything* we need. Colossians 2:10 tells us that we are *"complete in Him."* Ephesians 1:3 tells us that we are *"blessed with all spiritual blessings"* in Him. II Corinthians 2:14 assures us that we can always *"triumph in Christ,"* and in fact it is *"in Him we live, and move, and have our being"* (Acts 17:28).

In Christ we find total forgiveness, total identification, and total acceptance. Do we deserve or could we ever deserve these gifts of His love? Most certainly not. All we can do is graciously accept these gifts from Him in the same humble way we must accept His forgiveness for the penalty of our sins.

He loves us greatly, and He never makes His love conditional: "I'll love you if . . . ." or "I'll accept you if . . . ." Conditional love would enslave us to try to do things that we could never do in our own strength. But God wants us to know that He loves us completely and lives in us to give us His life and strength to do what we never could do without Him. We are "branches" and as such we can draw love and life directly from Him, our True Vine.

> And I have declared unto them Thy name, and will declare it: that the love wherewith Thou hast loved Me may be in them, and I in them (John 17:26).

Of course, with His love flowing into our lives, the natural outcome is that the Holy Spirit will produce His fruit in us. And Galatians 5:22 lets us know that "the fruit of the Spirit is love . . ." His love, the love that He lavishes on us, is to be poured out through us to others.

John 13:34-35 tells us that love for one another is the identifying mark that we are His. "A new commandment I give unto you, That ye love one another; as I have loved you, that ye also love one another. By this shall all men know that ye are my disciples, if ye have love one to another."

Now we know that loving some particular people isn't always easy. But, as with everything else in our new life, it's not something that we can do on our own. Thankfully, however, we can do it through Christ who strengthens us (Philippians 4:13). "And *the Lord make you to increase and abound in love* one toward another, and toward all men" (I Thessalonians 3:12).

> Herein is love, not that we loved God, but that He loved us, and sent His Son to be the propitiation for our sins. Beloved, if God so loved us, we ought also to love one another. No man hath seen God at any time. If we love one another, God dwelleth in us, and His love is perfected in us (I John 4:10-12).

Love isn't something that exists in a vacuum. It has effect. If it exists, it results in action. God so loved that *He gave.* And as Romans 8:32 puts it, "He that spared not His own Son, but delivered Him up for us all, how shall he not with Him also freely give us all things?" He is continuously giving, caring, directing, supplying—exercising His love in our lives. And yes, He is even chastening us in love, to mold and conform us to His likeness so that others may see His presence in us (Proverbs 3:11-12; Hebrews 12:6-7; Revelation 3:19).

As we learn to know the breadth and length and depth and height of God's love for us, what wonderful truths we find. He loves us with "an everlasting love" (Jeremiah 31:3). He loves us with a "great love" (Ephesians 2:4). His love never fails us. In love, He is rejoicing over us with joy and joying over us with singing (Zephaniah 3:17). Let us, in turn, rejoice in His wondrous love and let it flow through our lives!

a Song for fall

JESUS LOVES EVEN ME

I am so glad that our Father in heav'n
Tells of His love in the Book He has giv'n;
Wonderful things in the Bible I see—
This is the dearest, that Jesus loves me.

Tho' I forget Him and wander away,
Still He doth love me wherever I stray;
Back to His dear loving arms would I flee,
When I remember that Jesus loves me.

O if there's only one song I can sing
When in His beauty I see the great King,
This shall my song in eternity be:
"O what a wonder that Jesus loves me!"

I am so glad that Jesus loves me, Jesus loves me, Jesus loves me;
I am so glad that Jesus loves me, Jesus loves even me.

P. P. Bliss

selah time

1. What does it mean to you that Jesus loves you?

2. Isn't it wonderful that there is now no condemnation to you if you are in Christ! Reread Ephesians 1:4, and Colossians 1:21-22. Do you realize that as a Christian you are holy and without blame in God's sight?

3. Remembering the characteristics of God's love that we find in I Corinthians 13, what should your love toward others be like?

Chapter 9

A Song of Holiness

Rejoice in the LORD, O ye righteous: for praise is comely for the upright. Praise the LORD with the harp: sing unto Him with the psaltery and an instrument of ten strings. Sing unto Him a new song; play skilfully with a loud noise. For the word of the LORD is right; and all His works are done in truth. He loveth righteousness and judgment: the earth is full of the goodness of the LORD.

(PSALM 33:1-5)

Praise the Lord, His love is not dependent on our behavior. However, that fact certainly does not mean that our behavior does not matter (Romans 6:1-2). When we truly understand what Christ has done for us and how much He loves us, how could we disregard His claim on our lives? II Corinthians 5:14-15 says, "For the love of Christ constraineth [compels] us; because we thus judge, that if One died for all, then were all dead: And that He died for all, that they which live *should not henceforth live unto themselves, but unto Him* which died for them, and rose again."

So why is it that we so often find ourselves living for ourselves instead of for Him? The answers to that question could be many, but in simple form they boil down to the fact that we take our eyes off of Him and forget (or fail to understand) His great love for us. His love does compel us to allow Him to produce the fruit—the outcome in our lives—of holiness.

But now being made free from sin, and become servants to God, ye have your fruit unto holiness, and the end everlasting life (Romans 6:22).

a Song for Fall

I Thessalonians 4:3 tells us that "this is the will of God, even your sanctification." And verse 7 says that "God hath not called us unto uncleanness, but unto holiness." To be sanctified is to be made holy—set apart unto God.

There is a sense in which we were sanctified once for all at salvation, when we trusted Jesus Christ as our personal Savior to save us from the penalty of our sins. The blood of Christ washed our sins away so He could make us "holy and unblamable and unreprovable in His sight" (Colossians 1:21-22). But there is another sense in which sanctification is an ongoing process in our lives as we are conformed to the image of Christ day by day and moment by moment.

It is not God's will that our new life in Him should be characterized by sin. Rather, it should be a life of righteousness—conforming to His standard. Now it can't be our self-righteousness (the things we do in our own strength) because that can never please God (Isaiah 64:6; Romans 8:8). It has to be His righteousness—Christ's life lived in and through us by the power of the Holy Spirit. But how can we really experience that in our lives? God's Word has the answers.

> I beseech you therefore, brethren, by the mercies of God, that ye present your bodies a living sacrifice, holy, acceptable unto God, which is your reasonable service [worship]. And be not conformed to this world: but be ye transformed by the renewing of your mind, that ye may prove what is that good, and acceptable, and perfect, will of God (Romans 12:1-2).

These are very familiar verses to most of us. They've been the text of many sermons, and they certainly are full of truth and direction. Too often, however, we've been encouraged to focus entirely on the admonitions to be holy and not to be conformed to this world. The result has been that we're supposed to do this and this and this—do, do, do, do, do—and don't do a lot of other things. That's what I was caught up in for years—work, work, work—trying to be good and holy. Yes, Romans

12:1-2 are directing us to live in a holy manner, but we must also recognize the powerful motives and provisions that come with that admonition.

In the last chapter we emphasized God's wonderful love for us and the fact that through Christ we have found our true identity, complete forgiveness, and total acceptance. What mercy! What undeserved favor God has bestowed on us. And in light of His mercies, we can without reservation give ourselves to Him as a *living sacrifice*.

We don't have to die for our sin, because the Lamb of God was slain in our place; but the life that we now have should be sacrificed on the altar for God. This is death to self, that continuous surrender that we talked about in Chapter 4 (A Song of Deliverance). It is allowing Him to direct us, trusting Him to use us, and fully yielding to Him in all our ways. Romans 12:1 says that that is our "reasonable" service or worship in response to God's mercies.

And going on, we see that instead of being like the world, we are to be *transformed*. That word means "metamorphosed," a total change from one thing to another, similar to that which occurs when a caterpillar becomes a butterfly. (Did you know that when a caterpillar is metamorphosed in its cocoon, it doesn't just become a caterpillar that has sprouted wings? Its tissues break down and are restructured into a radically different adult insect, the butterfly.)

To make this amazing change something that we can truly experience, the Bible indicates that this transformation is *done to us*. We don't do it ourselves. God does the transforming!

And how is that transformation brought about? By the *renewing of our minds*. Remember how we discussed the battle for our minds in Chapter 7 (A Song of Peace)? There we looked at II Corinthians 10:5, "Casting down imaginations, and every high thing that exalteth itself against the knowledge of God, and bringing into captivity every thought to the obedience of Christ," and applied it specifically to thoughts that lead us to bitterness. Well, we need to apply it to other thoughts as well—all of our thoughts.

We need to allow God's Holy Spirit to constantly screen our thoughts and warn us of wrong ideas and attitudes. When the still small voice of God alerts us, we must turn to the Lord for His might to bring our thoughts into captivity. This ongoing process is the "renewing of our minds." And by offering ourselves as living sacrifices and allowing the continual renewing of our minds, we will find that Christ's holiness will become evident in our lives.

We can prove God's will for our lives. When we are renewed in the spirit of our minds and have God's perspective, Christlikeness will result. We will be proving moment by moment His "good, and acceptable, and perfect" will for our lives.

> That ye put off concerning the former conversation the old man, which is corrupt according to the deceitful lusts; And be renewed in the spirit of your mind; And that ye put on the new man, which after God is created in righteousness and true holiness (Ephesians 4:22-24).

You can't live the Christian life, and neither can I. We're dead! How much does a dead person do? Nothing! Absolutely nothing! But because we have the new life of Christ in us, we can choose to let Him live His life through us. That's "putting on the new man." But we must continually make that choice. We must exercise our "chooser" and deal with sin when He shows it to us (confess and repent to keep our fellowship with Him precious and unhindered). We must let His Word direct us and His Spirit guide us. We must say, "Yes, Lord, I choose Your will and Your way!"

> What? know ye not that your body is the temple of the Holy Ghost which is in you, which ye have of God, and ye are not your own? For ye are bought with a price: therefore glorify God in your body, and in your spirit, which are God's (I Corinthians 6:19-20).

Oh no! I'm not saying that we have to do, do, do! This is all about "being," not "doing." It's all about our relationship with our Savior. It's all about who we are in Christ. We are the *temple* of the Holy Spirit. He came to dwell in us the moment we were born again. We, in a real sense, are "buildings" owned and occupied by God. What we have to "do" is to be willing to allow Him to control His temple. He wants to use our bodies, which He bought with a price, to manifest His life here on earth.

Galatians 5:16 directs us to "walk in the Spirit, and [we will] not fulfil the lust of the flesh." And verse 25 in that same chapter says, "If we live in the Spirit, let us also walk in the Spirit." Between these two verses comes the description of the fruit of the Spirit: love, joy, peace, longsuffering, gentleness, goodness, faith, meekness, and temperance (Galatians 5:22-23).

For Christians, Christ is our life, and His indwelling Spirit is the power of our new life. We do live in the Spirit because He is in us, but we don't necessarily walk in the Spirit because we don't always let Him control our walk. Too often we try to walk in our own "wisdom" instead, disregarding His direction. The results are wrong attitudes and actions. But when we give way to His perfect rule, like the sap flowing from the vine through the branches, He produces His wonderful fruit in our lives—fruit in character with His holiness.

There is no middle of the road for us. We are either walking in the flesh, pitifully serving a destructive master that has no authority over us; or we are yielding ourselves to God to walk in His Spirit. We can't do both. It is either the one or the other (Galatians 5:16).

> Knowing this, that our old man is crucified with Him, that the body of sin might be destroyed, that henceforth we should not serve sin. For he that is dead is freed from sin. . . . Know ye not, that to whom ye yield yourselves servants to obey, his servants ye are to whom ye obey; whether of sin unto death, or of obedience unto righteousness? But God be thanked, that ye were the servants of sin, but ye have obeyed from the heart that form of doctrine which was delivered you. Being then made free from sin, ye became the servants of righteousness (Romans 6:6-7,16-18).

The good news is that we are free to be the servants of right-eousness. Romans 6 is a wonderful chapter that explains how we are dead to sin in fact, how we share the new life of Christ, and how we do the choosing of our master. We must consider ourselves, as we in truth are, dead to sin and alive to God (Romans 6:11).

What this means is that we must bow before our Lord and submit to Him rather than to the sin. As we choose to obey, we can claim the power to obey. The sins have no rightful hold on us. But we must recognize that fact and submit to our true Master. When we let sin ensnare us, we must confess it to God in brokenness and repentance.

The blood of Jesus Christ does not cleanse us from "mistakes." It cleanses us from sin confessed as sin! I John 1:9 says that "if we confess our sins, He is faithful and just to forgive us our sins, and to cleanse us from all unrighteousness." Confessing isn't just an emotional response, and neither is it just a passive statement of fact. You and I must have the same understanding that God has about any sin we commit. We must recognize that it (whatever sin it is) is so offensive to God that Jesus Christ had to become that sin and die on Calvary's cross to pay for its penalty and to save us from it (II Corinthians 5:21).

We can't have just a worldly sorrow for sin—crying in sorrow because we got caught. In response to the Spirit's convicting we will have a godly sorrow that brings about a true change in attitude—a turning away from that sin (II Corinthians 7:9-11). When you and I get to that point, we are letting Christ bring about that wonderful transformation into His image.

> And we know that all things work together for good to them that love God, to them who are the called according to His purpose. For whom He did foreknow, He also did *predestinate to be conformed to the image of His Son,* that He might be the firstborn among many brethren (Romans 8:28-29).

God has already determined that, as children of His, you and I are going to be conformed to the image of His Son. That's

His purpose for us—to be conformed to "Christlikeness." Right here in the nasty now-and-now, as we face life's trials and temptations, God is skillfully directing that glorious transformation.

Those struggles that we face, those failures that bring us low, those glimpses of His love and grace and mercy that we experience are all working together for our good and His glory. Let's not resist His guiding touch. Instead let us give way to His power and presence, allowing Him to produce that Christlikeness with its fruit of holiness in our lives.

God chose one small nation, the children of Israel, to show a difference between the holiness of God and the profanity of man. He wanted to show His glory through that people by having them understand and exhibit the character of their holy God. By doing so, they could stand in contrast to the sin-enslaved world around them.

And He wants to do exactly the same thing through you and me. He wants to use us to show a difference between the way He would respond in circumstances and the way the natural man would respond—between the holy (what He is like) and the profane (what man in the flesh is like). That's why He leaves us here after we are saved, to show His life through our lives. He doesn't need us to show our self-discipline, or our busyness, or our talents, or our do, do, doing and don't, don't, don'ting. It's Christ that the world needs to see in us.

> For the grace of God that bringeth salvation hath appeared to all men, Teaching us that, denying ungodliness and worldly lusts, we should live soberly, righteously, and godly, in this present world; Looking for that blessed hope, and the glorious appearing of the great God and our Saviour Jesus Christ; who gave Himself for us, that He might redeem us from all iniquity, and purify unto Himself a peculiar people, zealous of good works (Titus 2:11-14).

We can't produce holiness in our lives, but praise God, He can. The same grace that brought us salvation also enables us to live our new lives in Christ. Yes, we were saved by grace, but we are also sanctified, purified, and conformed to the image of Christ in that ongoing transformation *by grace*. Our own works can't bring it about. Trusting and submitting to our God, who loves us so, allows Him to bring it about. When we embrace that blessed Vine-and-branch relationship with Him, He will produce holy fruit.

NOTHING BETWEEN

Nothing between my soul and the Savior,
Naught of this world's delusive dream;
I have renounced all sinful pleasure,
Jesus is mine; there's nothing between.

Nothing between, like worldly pleasure,
Habits of life though harmless they seem,
Must not my heart from Him e'er sever,
He is my all; there's nothing between.

Nothing between, like pride or station,
Self or friends shall not intervene,
Tho' it may cost me much tribulation,
I am resolved; there's nothing between.

Nothing between, e'en many hard trials,
Tho' the whole world against me convene;
Watching with prayer and much self-denial,
I'll triumph at last, with nothing between.

Nothing between my soul and the Savior,
So that His blessed face may be seen;
Nothing preventing the least of His favor,
Keep the way clear! Let nothing between.

C. A. Tindley
Copyright, 1905, by C. A. Tindley

 *selah time*

1. Think about what it means that God transforms us on the inside so that what we "do" outwardly springs from what He has already done and continues to do inwardly.

2. God bought us with a price, and our bodies are His. What does it mean, then, that our eyes are His eyes? Our ears are His ears? Our lips are His lips? Our hands are His hands? etc.

3. Is there "nothing between" your soul and the Savior?

Chapter 10

A SONG OF CONTENTMENT

And let the peace of God rule in your hearts, to the which also
ye are called in one body; and be ye thankful. Let the word of
Christ dwell in you richly in all wisdom; teaching and
admonishing one another in psalms and hymns and spiritual
songs, singing with grace in your hearts to the Lord.

(COLOSSIANS 3:15-16)

Although we have been touching on many varied topics, I hope you are noticing that the only "Song" that can bring "harmony" to our lives is our Lord Jesus. Only He can calm our troubles. Only He can soothe our sorrows. Only He can compose a divine symphony in and through our lowly "instruments." It is our precious relationship with Him, in which we are ever growing in understanding, and in trust, and in likeness to Him, that produces a wonderful melody in our lives. It is that relationship that brings us true contentment.

> Not that I speak in respect of want: for I have learned, in whatsoever state I am, therewith to be content. I know both how to be abased, and I know how to abound: every where and in all things I am instructed both to be full and to be hungry, both to abound and to suffer need. I can do all things through Christ which strengtheneth me (Philippians 4:11-13).

Contentment is not something we are born with. And we can't muster it up by our own will power either. This instructive passage in Philippians gives us two important clues about contentment: it is something we must *learn,* and we learn it *through Christ* "in whom are hid all the treasures of wisdom and knowledge" (Colossians 2:3).

Okay, that seems pretty basic to most of us who have read Philippians a few times. We are prone to mentally say, "yes, that's right," as we think momentarily of some instances in our lives when we've been abased and when we've abounded. We probably learned something about how to be content through those experiences, and so we file that bit of Scriptural truth away in the back of our minds and go on. However, you and I are not going to file it away right now. We need to find out how it really applies to us, right here, right now, where we live.

To illustrate what I mean, I'm going to use a circumstance in my life as an example. I am single. For those of you reading this who are single, I don't have to tell you how this can relate to contentment. But just in case you married folks don't know, being single isn't exactly an easy way to live. In a manner of speaking, it is a major "tribulation" to many of us who find ourselves in that state.

But undoubtedly you too have at least one major "tribulation" in your life—whether it is being single, or being in a difficult marriage, or having a physical problem, or whatever. You know the circumstance in your life that most often troubles you. If you think about all the "problems" or "disadvantages" you face because of that circumstance, it can certainly leave you discontented.

For the next few pages, I'm going to deal specifically with some Scriptural principles that have helped me find contentment as a single. If being single is not your "tribulation," however, don't pass over this chapter. You will find that many of these thoughts have plenty of application for you regardless of the difficult circumstances you face.

> And we know that the Son of God is come, and hath given us an understanding, that we may know Him that is true, and we are in Him that is true, even in

His Son Jesus Christ. This is the true God, and eternal life (I John 5:20).

First, single or married, we must understand that our wonderful, life-giving relationship with our Lord is not an occasional pastime. We've discussed that relationship in earlier chapters, but here I want to sum up our part in keeping a revival relationship with our Lord with the thoughts of three familiar hymns. He has often used these hymns to remind me of that attitude of brokenness that draws us and keeps us close to our dear Savior.

We must live "Moment By Moment" (p. 49). It is "in Him we live, and move, and have our being" (Acts 17:28). If He chooses to take our breath at any given moment, that's His business. But we must ask ourselves what we are doing with the breath He is giving us right now at this moment. We can face life moment by moment, and we can allow Christ to live through us moment by moment. In so doing, we will also learn contentment moment by moment.

And as we live moment by moment, we must be able to say that there is "Nothing Between My Soul and the Savior" (p. 96). As the sap flows naturally through a branch, we must abide in Christ and have nothing in our lives which would hinder the Holy Spirit's work in and through us. He can and will produce precious fruit in our lives when there's nothing between. And the fruit of the Spirit, which includes the characteristics of love and joy and peace, is an essential part of contentment.

Then, regardless of our circumstances, our relationships, our possessions, we must be willing to say, "I Surrender All" (p. 132). We can't withhold anything from God and still find contentment. When we relinquish control and stop making demands, we'll discover His amazing ability to satisfy the desires of our heart (Psalm 37:4).

For this thing I besought the Lord thrice, that it might depart from me. And He said unto me, "My grace is sufficient for thee: for My strength is made perfect in weakness." Most gladly therefore will I rather glory in my infirmities, that the power of Christ may rest upon me. Therefore I take pleasure in infirmities, in reproaches, in necessities, in persecutions, in distresses for Christ's sake: for when I am weak, then am I strong (II Corinthians 12:8-10).

I know that I am called to be single today, because I am! I had several opportunities to marry, but the Lord closed the doors every time. If, down the road of my earthly life, the Lord chooses to change my marital status, that's fine. But if not, His grace is sufficient for me! I have to realize that the Person (Christ) who said that to Paul also says it to me. He will prove Himself to be my all-sufficiency at every moment of every day and in whatever difficulty I may face.

It is easy for us singles to start thinking, "Why doesn't anybody love me?" "Why doesn't anybody want me?" "Why doesn't God let me get married?" "Lord, it's not fair!" "I don't understand!" "Woe is me!" But then, any difficult circumstance can lead to those kinds of "why" questions.

Where is our focus when we are thinking those thoughts and asking why? It's on ourselves—me, me, me, and I, I, I! But the victory and joy in our relationship with the Lord comes when we choose to focus not on us but on Him.

"And we know that all things work together for good to them that love God, to them who are the called according to *His purpose*" (Romans 8:28). We don't have to understand. But we must acknowledge Him as God and know that He understands why and what His purpose is in this circumstance. We must acknowledge that He is working in us "both to will and to do of His good pleasure" (Philippians 2:13).

It is *His purpose* He is working out in us, yet so often we try to overrule Him and work out our own agendas. We can't do that and be content. We are not here for ourselves. We were "bought with a price" and therefore we should glorify God in our bodies and in our spirits because they are God's (I Corinthians 6:20).

My body is God's body, and He can do with it what He wants, when He wants, and where He wants. I just need to give in. That's hard to do because of my pride. But when I do, I find that His grace is sufficient, and peace and contentment are the results.

> And God is able to make all grace abound toward you;
> that ye, always having all sufficiency in all things, may
> abound to every good work (II Corinthians 9:8).

His grace is so sufficient that we can "glory in" and "take pleasure in" our difficulties, even persecutions and distresses. The jokes, the loneliness, and other things can hurt, but even in the difficulties we can give thanks (I Thessalonians 5:18). When we do that, we are learning to be content with who we are in Christ.

We are learning that in our weakness we can let Him be our strength and our sufficiency. We are not able to cope with problems, much less overcome them. But *He is able* to be our sufficiency in all things! When we realize that, we can have the peace of God that passes all understanding and keeps our hearts and minds through Christ Jesus (Philippians 4:7).

> This I say then, Walk in the Spirit, and ye shall not
> fulfil the lust of the flesh. For the flesh lusteth against
> the Spirit, and the Spirit against the flesh: and these
> are contrary the one to the other: so that ye cannot
> do the things that ye would (Galatians 5:16-17).

I'm certainly not proud of this fact, but before I was saved I was into pornography. After I accepted Christ as my personal Savior, the books, the people, and everything associated with it were gone—I was indeed a new creature in Christ. Even so, the thoughts would still return.

When I was tempted to think on those things, the Holy Spirit was saying to me, "Wilma! What are you thinking?" Immediately I knew that my Savior would not think such thoughts. I had to make the choice of either dwelling on those thoughts or thinking the way that God said I should. I had to "put off concerning the former [lifestyle] the old man, which is corrupt according to the deceitful lusts; And be renewed in the spirit of [my] mind" (Ephesians 4:22-23).

As a young Christian, I didn't understand then how dependent I must be on Christ's strength to overcome sin. But nevertheless I did yield to Him and did choose to think on right things (Philippians 4:8)—things that would please Him. I found, too, that He was faithful to me and that His peace did indeed keep my heart and mind when I turned to Him. Contentment could never come by giving in to sin, but it could grow as my relationship with my Lord deepened.

Life is tough today. Everywhere you look there are inducements to think impure thoughts—television, magazines, billboards, etc. And we have normal, natural physical desires. Those desires are God-given and good within His bounds, but we must be ever-dependent on Him to be our sufficiency and strength when we are tempted to sin. When we're faced with those temptations we must "nip them in the bud" by choosing to think pure thoughts and choosing to turn off, throw out, tune out, or otherwise "flee" the devil's snares (II Timothy 2:22). God's grace will be sufficient immediately.

> Let love be without [hypocrisy]. Abhor that which is evil; cleave to that which is good. Be kindly affectioned one to another with brotherly love; in honour preferring one another (Romans 12:9-10).

Another key principle for learning contentment as a single is to nurture quality relationships in our lives. There are many times when we all need to be alone with our Lord, but that fact does not rule out a large measure of social contact in our lives. We aren't cut out to be hermits. And though we as singles may lack the special relationship one has with a spouse, we can and should have quality relationships with others—friends and family members—as God gives us opportunity.

There is, however, a critical rule for all relationships. We won't find contentment in any relationship if we are in it for what we can get out of it. Selfishness will breed misery. Galatians 5:14 tells us that we should love our neighbor as our-selves. Romans 12:10 goes further to tell us that we should put the interests of others before our own, and Philippians 2:3 says that we should esteem others better than ourselves. Remember I Corinthians 13:5 reveals that God's love doesn't seek its own, and it is His unselfish love that should shine through us.

> And whatsoever ye do, do it heartily, as to the Lord, and not unto men; Knowing that of the Lord ye shall receive the reward of the inheritance: for ye serve the Lord Christ (Colossians 3:23-24).

Therefore, we can't be hypocritical and self-serving in our friendships, reaching out only to those we think will help us in return, to those we want to meet our needs. When we are serv-ing others to get something in return, we're going to be disap-pointed and perhaps become bitter. When people don't meet our expectations, the poochie lip comes out, revealing the self-centeredness of our actions. That's why we must keep our eyes on the Lord instead of on other people. Our "expectations" must be from Him (Psalm 62:5).

That truth was certainly brought home to me a few years ago when a good friend of mine had not lived up to my expec-tations. I remember driving down the road on my way to a speaking engagement all the while telling the Lord how "disap-pointed" I was in that person and how she needed His help. But I was the one that was irritated. I was sore. I was down-right frustrated.

While there, someone gave me the following thought on humility. I had hardly begun to read it when I saw the word "disappointed" on the fourth line. I gasped, knowing that the Lord was drawing this reading to my attention in a very per-sonal way. The thoughts went right to my heart. And the next day I ended up crying all the way as I drove back home.

Do you have a troubled relationship with someone? See if the Lord is trying to teach you a lesson in humility just as He did me.

HUMILITY

Humility is perfect quietness of heart.
It is for me to have no trouble.
It is never to fret or be vexed or irritated,
sore or disappointed.
It is to expect nothing, to wonder at nothing that is
done to me, to feel nothing that is done against me.
It is to be at rest when nobody praises me, or when
I am blamed or despised.
It is to have a blessed home in the Lord,
where I can go in and shut the door and
kneel to my Father in secret, where I am
at peace as in a deep sea of calmness when
all around and above is trouble.
It is the fruit of the Lord Jesus Christ's
redemptive work on Calvary's cross, made
manifest to those who are His own and who
are definitely subjected to the Holy Spirit.

Anonymous

I have a copy of that thought in my car, and I keep other copies in handy places. I find that I need frequent reminders because thoughts about how other people "disappoint" me can creep in easily. And if they do, I need to let the Holy Spirit have His way in my heart and in my mind, taking my focus away from myself.

Instead of focusing on ourselves, we should be unselfishly looking to meet the needs of others. We can't stay cocooned in our own little world expecting others to come and satisfy us. And we can't be reaching out so that we can get praise, appreciation, or other "paybacks" in return. Christ told us that He "came not to be ministered unto, but to minister" (Matthew 20:28), and He tells us to do likewise.

While we should nurture relationships that honor the Lord, we must remember that no human relationship can fill the deep longings of our hearts. It is knowing our Savior and cultivating our relationship with Him that truly brings contentment. If we look for it in people, we will always be disappointed. But when we seek it in Him, we will be satisfied (Psalm 63:1-5).

> Wherefore, my brethren, ye also are become dead to the law by the body of Christ; that ye should be married to Another, even to Him who is raised from the dead, that we should bring forth fruit unto God (Romans 7:4).

No, I don't know all the reasons why God has chosen to keep me single. But I do know some of them. In I Corinthians 7:34-35 Paul says that an unmarried woman can care for the things of the Lord *without distraction.* That certainly doesn't mean that it is wrong for a woman to be married and have the distractions of meeting the needs of a husband and children. But it does mean that a single person has the freedom to serve the Lord in ways that a married person can't or can't as easily.

Through Phebe Ministries the Lord has given me the opportunity to travel extensively, ministering to women in churches and in Christian camps and in homes. I can let God direct my schedule, my finances, and my time without having to consider a husband or children. That freedom lets me have some unusual opportunities to minister.

I often stay in homes as I travel across America. There I find many women needing help with the laundry or the dishes as well as a word of encouragement from the Lord. By pitching in with the work, I have many opportunities to counsel and even share the gospel.

Recently, a lady told me about an unsaved Catholic friend of hers who wanted to talk with me. However, that friend was busy painting her dining room, getting it ready for vacationing relatives due to arrive the next day. Well, I went to see the friend anyway. When she came to the door and I told her who I was, she said, "Oh! Do I have a lot of questions for you! But I've got company coming and I'm painting my dining room and . . . !"

I interrupted her and said, "Your friend told me that, so I brought my paintclothes with me. I have them out in the car. Let me run and get them."

I turned around and ran to my car, leaving her with her mouth open. I got my paintclothes, and we painted all day together. I was able to answer her questions while we painted. She didn't receive Christ as her Savior that day, but it was a positive contact, sowing the seed of the gospel in her life.

Now you don't have to have a ministry like mine with Phebe to have special opportunities of service in your life. I know the Lord has given me this ministry as a single for His purposes, and I thank Him for the freedom I have with which to serve Him. Whatever your circumstances are, the Lord has with them also given you opportunities to minister. We can find much joy and learn contentment as we explore the opportunities He gives us to serve Him and others.

> Blessed be God, even the Father of our Lord Jesus Christ, the Father of mercies, and the God of all comfort; who comforteth us in all our tribulation, that we may be able to comfort them which are in any trouble, by the comfort wherewith we ourselves are comforted of God (II Corinthians 1:3-4).

In addition, the Lord has given me many opportunities to minister to other single ladies. God expects us to share the comfort we receive from Him with others. It's hard for a married woman to give much spiritual comfort to a discontented single woman. It's hard for someone who has never experienced the loss of a spouse to comfort a grieving widow. It's hard for someone who does not know the distresses of divorce to comfort someone dealing with a divorce.

When we learn contentment through our troubles, we have a special God-given gift of hope and encouragement that we can share. Broken to accept His will in our lives, we find our sufficiency in Him. And then our all-sufficient God wants to use us to show forth His mercy and grace to others.

But let patience have her perfect work, that ye may be perfect and entire, wanting nothing (James 1:4).

Regardless of how or why we are single (or disabled, or disadvantaged, or whatever), we have to get away from the "poochie lip disease"! Our God has promised to "supply *all our need* according to His riches in glory by Christ Jesus" (Philippians 4:19). James tells us that we can be complete, lacking nothing. We can have absolute contentment in any situation.

Things may seem crazy in our lives, and we don't understand what God is doing. But He is not trying our patience. He is trying our faith. He is trying (testing) our absolute dependence on Him, our trust in Him to manage our lives. We can complain, we can panic, we can rebel—or we can trust. And when we learn to trust, we find true contentment in Him. Then His peace will rule in our hearts, we can be thankful, and we can sing with grace in our hearts to Him (Colossians 3:15-16).

IS YOUR ALL ON THE ALTAR?

You have longed for sweet peace, and for faith to increase,
And have earnestly, fervently prayed;
But you cannot have rest or be perfectly blest
Until all on the altar is laid.

Would you walk with the Lord, in the light of His Word,
And have peace and contentment alway?
You must do His sweet will, to be free from all ill,
On the altar your all you must lay.

Oh, we never can know what the Lord will bestow
Of the blessings for which we have prayed,
Till our body and soul He doth fully control,
And our all on the altar is laid.

Who can tell all the love He will send from above,
And how happy our hearts will be made,
Of the fellowship sweet we shall share at His feet,
When our all on the altar is laid.

A Song for Fall

Is your all on the altar of sacrifice laid?
Your heart, does the Spirit control?
You can only be blest and have peace and sweet rest,
As you yield Him your body and soul.

Elisha A. Hoffman

selah time

1. What is the most difficult circumstance or "tribulation" in your life right now?

2. Are you seeking contentment from a person or from something else rather than from the Lord?

3. Are you disappointed in someone right now and feeling hurt? Reread the thoughts on humility (p. 106).

4. If you are single, are you willing to serve the Lord with the unique opportunities He gives you? And are you willing to trust Him to meet your physical, emotional, spiritual, and financial needs in His way and in His time?

a Song for Winter

Winter is a time . . . of quiet reflection; . . . of still and crisp cold and white and clean snow; . . . of celebration, enjoyment, and expectation.

~

When our lives may seem to be mostly a flurry of activity, we should treasure the quiet moments or seasons that give us opportunity for reflection. They are times for communion; they are times for cleansing; they are times for enjoying the warmth of God's presence.

As the burdens and cares and activities of this life surround us, may we ever seek quiet retreats with our Savior. May we find ourselves in the midst of every season resting and rejoicing in Him.

~

Chapter 11

A SONG OF REST

Yet the LORD will command His lovingkindness in the daytime, and in the night His song shall be with me, and my prayer unto the God of my life.

(PSALM 42:8)

Psalm 46:10 says, "Be still, and know that I am God." I have written in my Bible by that verse, "and not you, Wilma!" It is so very easy for us to think we know how things ought to be—what should be happening in our life, what other people should be doing, how God should be working out certain circumstances, etc. And when we think we have things figured out, we act on our assumptions . . . and end up discouraged, dismayed, and weary.

God wants to be the God of our lives. He knows all about our lives and the lives of those around us. He knows about the circumstances we face. So often we worry and we scurry about trying to take care of everything ourselves, when what we really need to do is be still and find our rest in Him.

> Come unto Me, all ye that labour and are heavy laden, and I will give you rest. Take My yoke upon you, and learn of Me: for I am meek and lowly in heart: and ye shall find rest unto your souls. For My yoke is easy, and My burden is light (Matthew 11:28-30).

Before we discuss the wonderful rest that our Lord promises to us in these verses, do you know what a yoke is? It's a wooden frame that is used to harness a pair of animals together, so that they can do a job like pulling a plow or a wagon. When we get in Christ's yoke, we are in the place where we are available for His use and ready to hear and obey His commands.

In His yoke we can "press toward the [goal] for the prize of the high calling of God in Christ Jesus" (Philippians 3:14). That goal is knowing Christ and becoming Christ-like. As you may know, a farmer plowing has to keep his eye on the goal at the end of the field. If, instead, he looks down and watches the ground he's plowing, he'll plow a crooked furrow. It's no different for us. We must keep our eyes on our goal—not on all the current circumstances of our lives—or we'll get off track.

Christ commands that we get in His yoke, but we're not in it alone. I believe the Holy Spirit, the Paraclete, as the One who comes along side, is there with us in Christ's yoke. He's there all the time with that still small voice saying, "Wilma, 'this is the way, walk ye in it, when ye turn to the right hand, and when ye turn to the left'" (Isaiah 30:21). He's saying, "Wilma, don't look down at that 'furrow' you're plowing. Look toward the goal—Christ."

> Thou wilt keep him in perfect peace, whose mind is stayed on thee: because he trusteth in Thee. Trust ye in the LORD for ever: for in the LORD JEHOVAH is everlasting strength (Isaiah 26:3-4).

All right, so what does being in a yoke have to do with rest? After all, a yoke is an implement for work, isn't it? Yes, but the emphasis is on whose yoke we're in. That makes all the difference.

A few years ago a pastor friend of mine was struggling. He was laboring and heavy laden, trying to do and be many things. In the process his Christian life as well as his ministry had lost its joy. While he was driving down the highway late one night, tears were streaming down his cheeks. He hardly knew how to pray, but he pleaded with the Lord for some kind of help in his despair.

There in that dark night, the Lord brought Matthew 11:28-30 to his mind. "Come unto Me, all ye that labour and are heavy laden, and I will give you rest. Take My yoke upon you . . . ." *Take My yoke!* There was the answer! He was so busy, so tired, and so discouraged, trying to do all the things that Christian leaders expected of him, those things that other people expected of him, and especially those things that he expected of himself. That night he realized that he was trying to wear a yoke that wasn't Christ's yoke. It was a yoke that was hard and heavy and impossible to bear.

The fact that it is *Christ's yoke* we are supposed to be wearing can give us an incredible freedom and, yes, rest. During the course of our Christian lives we so often accumulate staggering lists of do's and don'ts, and we try, try, try to live up to them. Well-meaning pastors, evangelists, and Bible teachers stress things we should be doing so that we will please God. (And I was certainly guilty of stressing those things to ladies for several years.) We take the admonitions to heart, working hard at our Christianity, but becoming increasingly burdened.

We have already dealt with part of the problem in earlier chapters. That is the fact that too often we try to live the Christian life in our own strength rather than claiming the life of Christ within us. We can't live in our own strength. We must live in His. We can't forget that and still find rest. We'll come back to this thought shortly.

But there is often another problem that makes the loads we bear seem so heavy. And that is that we've gotten in a yoke pulling loads Christ never intended for us to bear. Quite often we've set up all kinds of expectations for our Christian lives, and those expectations tend to make our lives miserable. Why? Living for Christ shouldn't make our lives miserable, should it? Of course not. But the simple fact is that in the process of trying to meet all those expectations, we usually lose sight of Christ. We take on a yoke that isn't His.

Now, before we look at this further, I need to make this point very clear. Submitting to Christ's yoke will keep us following Biblical standards for our lives. We cannot find His rest while rejecting His clear commands for our lives. But Christ points out that *His yoke* is easy and *His burden* is light. In I John 5:3 we

read that "this is the love of God, that we keep His commandments: and His commandments are not grievous [burdensome]."

But while we realize that Christ's yoke will keep us in a path
following His commandments, we do need to examine the expectations we've accumulated in our lives and check them according
to two telling criteria. The first is, as it should be, "Is this expectation I've taken upon myself a clear command of Scripture for
me?" For instance, I know that being morally pure, loving others,
and attending church is God's will for me because the Bible tells
me so (I Thessalonians 4:3; I Thessalonians 4:9; Hebrews 10:25).

And the other is, if there is no clear Scriptural guideline,
"Am I sure that it is Christ making this demand of me?" We can
pile up lots of burdensome expectations in attempts to win
God's blessing or man's praise. We may "work, work, work" out
of a sense of duty or obligation. Yet, reasons such as these
make the goals a heavy and frustrating burden for us to carry.
When we fail to meet our goals, we feel discouraged and guilty,
and when we do meet them they often don't bring the joy that
serving our Lord should bring.

Our overriding goal in these areas should simply be to do
what God wants us to do. We, as individuals, must seek the
Lord's guidance for us in these areas. We can't live up to everyone else's convictions. But God's grace is sufficient for us to
live as the Lord leads us personally. And He will never lead us
contrary to the clear teaching of His written Word.

Jesus is the Way (John 14:6)—He does not just show us
the way. He is in us, and He will make His will known to us if
we are willing to receive it. If we are allowing Him to be our
life, Romans 12:2 indicates that we will "prove what is that
good, and acceptable, and perfect, will of God." And Philippians 2:13 makes it clear that it is "God which worketh in [us]
both to will and to do of His good pleasure."

The Lord wants a strong and open relationship with us in
which He can communicate and live His life in and through us.
Sure, we may be busy, but it won't be busyness in "self-deter-
mined" causes in which we labor in our own strength. Instead

it will be us pursuing Christ's purposes in His strength. In His yoke the still small voice will be our constant guide, the yoke will be easy to bear, and the burden will be light.

> There remaineth therefore a rest to the people of God. For he that is entered into His rest, he also hath ceased from his own works, as God did from His. Let us labour therefore to enter into that rest, lest any man fall after the same example of unbelief (Hebrews 4:9-11).

God created the heavens and the earth in six days, as recorded in Genesis, and on the seventh day He rested. His creation work was complete. And as He rested on the seventh day from creating the world, we too can have rest today because the redemptive work of Jesus Christ is complete. You and I can rest in the total cleansing we received at Calvary. You and I can stop working and trusting in our own efforts and start trusting in God's finished work.

But I know what you may be thinking. "Now, Wilma, look at what verse 11 says. 'Let us labour therefore . . .' I thought you said that we couldn't do anything to live the Christ-life, but it says there that we have to labor. We have to keep working!"

It's been a wonderful encouragement for me to learn that that word "labour" in verse 11 denotes more of an attitude than an action. It is not a "get out there and work to do it!" Rather it means to be excited and anticipate what God is going to do in any given situation because I can't do anything. I am to rest. I am to cease from my labors. I am to let go and let God live His life in and through me.

> For thus saith the Lord GOD, the Holy One of Israel; In returning and rest shall ye be saved; in quietness and in confidence shall be your strength . . . . (Isaiah 30:15).

If we don't let God live His life in us, we're going to try to live the Christian life in our own strength. What a wearisome task! And all we'll ever accomplish is wood, hay, and stubble (I Corinthians 3:11-15).

Hebrews 4 reminds us of how the children of Israel failed to believe God's promise and conquer the land of Canaan. Instead of claiming God's promised victory, they wandered wearily in the wilderness for forty years. Why did the children of Israel not go into the land? Verse 11 says that it was because of the sin of unbelief. God says that we are dead and our lives are hid with Christ in God. Do we really believe Him, or are we still trying to live the Christian life on our own? We must stop *trying* and start *trusting* Christ to live His life in and through us.

> Commit thy way unto the LORD; trust also in Him; and He shall bring it to pass. And He shall bring forth thy righteousness as the light, and thy judgment as the noonday. Rest in the LORD, and wait patiently for Him . . . . (Psalm 37:5-7).

We are justified by faith, but once we are saved, the just are supposed to live by faith, too! (Habakkuk 2:4; Romans 1:17; Galatians 3:11; Hebrews 10:38) The faith that believed that Christ could wash away our sins is the same kind of faith we need to let Him be the Lord of our lives. When we have that kind of total faith in Him, we find rest. We can cast all of our care on Him because He cares for us (I Peter 5:7). We can't handle all the trials, cares, and responsibilities of this life, but we can place our complete faith and trust in our loving and powerful Lord. He is our life; He is our strength; and in Him we can have rest—a rest of faith.

A few years ago I told my friend Polly, "You know, Polly, when I was saved I had a lot of four-letter words in my vocabulary. But just overnight, the Lord changed my language. However, I did keep one of those words."

She looked at me with some hesitation, took a deep breath, and asked, "Which one?"

I said, "Help!"

We constantly need God's help, but His "help" is not mere assistance. I had to learn that it's not, "Lord, help me to . . . ." It's just "Lord, help!" "I" can't do anything. I am dead—crucified with Christ. But the Christ who lives in me can. When I stop trying to figure things out and work things out and take care of everything with just a smidgen of help (assistance) from God, I free Him to be God in my life. I can rest in His wisdom and ability to take care of things. And I am free simply to allow Him to lead me and use me as He knows best.

There's a common saying around. You've probably seen it on refrigerator magnets or little plaques. It goes, "Lord! Help me to remember that nothing is going to happen to me today that You and I together can't handle!" I'm sorry, but that thought is just plain wrong. *He* is the only One capable of handling the things that happen to us. When we try to handle them "together" with Him, we louse things up.

But when we have the faith to entrust the workings of our lives to Him—when we trust Him as the God of our lives, we find Him faithful. We learn that it has to be His labor, not ours; His strength, not ours; His yoke, not ours; His life, not ours. And in that realization we find a haven of sweet rest, safe and secure while the waves and tempests of life roll.

JESUS, I AM RESTING

Jesus, I am resting, resting In the joy of what Thou art;
I am finding out the greatness Of Thy loving heart.
Thou hast bid me gaze upon Thee, And Thy beauty fills my soul,
For by Thy transforming power, Thou hast made me whole.

Simply trusting Thee, Lord Jesus, I behold Thee as Thou art,
And Thy love, so pure, so changeless, Satisfies my heart;
Satisfies its deepest longings, Meets, supplies its ev'ry need,
Compasseth me round with blessings: Thine is love indeed!

Ever lift Thy face upon me, As I work and wait for Thee;
Resting 'neath Thy smile, Lord Jesus, Earth's dark shadows flee.
Brightness of my Father's glory, Sunshine of my Father's face,
Keep me ever trusting, resting, Fill me with Thy grace.

Jesus, I am resting, resting, In the joy of what Thou art,
I am finding out the greatness Of Thy loving heart.

Jean Sophie Pigott

selah time

1. Examine the "yoke" that you are wearing and the burdens you are trying to carry in your Christian life. Is it Christ's yoke, and are they His burdens?

2. Recognizing that "the just shall live by faith" (notice it's not by works), look up Hebrews 11:6 and Romans 14: 23b. What do they indicate about our self-efforts to live the Christian life?

3. Do you find yourself asking for the Lord's "assistance" rather than depending on Him totally as your all-sufficiency?

Chapter 12

A Song of Joyful Abandon

I will sing unto the LORD as long as I live: I will sing praise to
my God while I have my being. My meditation of Him shall be
sweet: I will be glad in the LORD.

(PSALM 104:33-34)

Psalm 43:4 speaks of "God my exceeding joy." Learning who our God is and who we are in Him does indeed bring joy to our lives. But we will never know the depths of that wonderful joy personally while we are trying to hang on to the control of our lives. When, however, we abandon control to our loving and sovereign Lord, we will find Him faithful to all of His promises. We will find Him to be all-sufficient. We will find Him as our exceeding joy. An amazing life awaits us as we yield to Him in joyful abandon.

Psalm 132:9 says "let Thy saints shout *for joy*." That's exactly what I want to do—shout for joy as I see the Lord working not only in my life but also in the lives of others. In my autobiography, *Sister of Mercy,* I mentioned that I had been asking the Lord to show me what it means that "God so loved" not just the world, but me personally. Many of the thoughts that I've tried to share with you in this book are a part of the amazing lessons that have resulted. And over the last two years they've culminated in the awesome realization that God is and must be sovereign—absolute ruler in control of everything in my life—and that He is my all-sufficient One.

Because of these two truths, *abandon* is a good word to sum up what the joyful Christian life is all about. First of all, we find joy in our Christian lives by abandoning a life lived our way in our own strength, to live instead *in Christ*. We can't live the Christian life. We're crucified with Christ. We must by faith let Him live in and through us with His strength. I know we've come back to this basic point again and again, but we're all so prone to forget. We have to give up—die to self and put our lives completely in our Lord's hands. In doing so, we give in to His sovereignty.

And secondly, we should abandon our cares to trust in God's promises because we will always find Him sufficient for us in every way. "Casting all your care upon Him; for He careth for you" (I Peter 5:7). Scripture assures us of the certainties of God's love for us, of His power to save us, and of His constant care and provision for our needs. "But my God shall supply all your need according to His riches in glory by Christ Jesus" (Philippians 4:19). He is ever faithful to His Word. We cannot cling to doubts and fears and still expect to experience His joy. We can and we must by faith believe Him.

> Wherefore, if God so clothe the grass of the field, which to day is, and to morrow is cast into the oven, shall He not much more clothe you, O ye of little faith? Therefore take no thought, saying, What shall we eat? or, What shall we drink? or, Wherewithal shall we be clothed? (For after all these things do the Gentiles seek:) for your heavenly Father knoweth that ye have need of all these things. But seek ye first the kingdom of God, and His righteousness; and all these things shall be added unto you (Matthew 6:30-33).

The God of creation, who feeds the sparrows and clothes the flowers, knows every need of our lives. He tells us that our petty concerns, which we so often let dominate our thoughts, should always take a back seat to what is really important— God's reign in our hearts and lives. When we allow Him to control our life circumstances and when we allow His righteousness to work through us, everything else will fall into place. We can trust Him to be our all-sufficient One!

> Faithful is He that calleth you, who also will do it (I
> Thessalonians 5:24).

For years I've been amazed to see how faithfully the Lord
has met my every need. Ten years ago I left a steady job to go
out as a missionary in Catholic evangelism. I remember praying
at six o'clock in the morning the day I set out on my first jour-
ney, "Father! I know beyond a shadow of a doubt that You have
called me to do what I'm setting out to do. Now by faith I am
obeying Your call. But You know that I have only $95 a month
in promised support."

At that point I Thessalonians 5:24 came into my mind. As I
drove that day from South Carolina to Pennsylvania, He kept
reassuring me that He indeed is my Father and that He would
take care of me as His daughter. At that time He also impressed
upon me that I should not ask for financial support, but that I
should simply trust Him to meet all of my needs. From that day
until this, He has never failed to provide for me through the
abundant generosity of fellow Christians. Financially and in
every other way, He has proved over and over again that He is
my sufficiency.

Because He is sovereign and because He is all-sufficient, I
can abandon myself to Him. I don't have to worry about
whether I'm giving up too much or whether or not the results
are worthwhile. I can confidently lose my life for His sake
(Matthew 10:39). His love for me is *so* great that for me to do
His will will always be my richest joy. With David I can say, "I
delight to do Thy will, O my God" (Psalm 40:8).

> And ye shall know the truth, and the truth shall make
> you free (John 8:32).

As I've come to understand more and more of what Christ
in love has done for me, I've found a joyous freedom in Him. It
is a freedom from the guilt, condemnation, and penalty of my
sin (Romans 8:1). It is a freedom that sets me apart from sin to
serve my Lord (Romans 6:22). And it's a freedom from a life

lived by law, allowing me instead to live every moment by grace through faith and in the joy of His love (Galatians 5:1).

Over a year ago I asked the Lord to let me see these truths of His Word at work in the lives of others. It's been a thrill for me to watch and see, time and again, as He has given me opportunity to share with ladies, that these truths are setting them free as well. What a blessing to see the Lord give them the same joy and peace and contentment in their lives that He has given me. And it hasn't stopped there. Those ladies are turning around and helping other people to understand these wonderful truths. That brings me joy—absolute sheer joy! He is just so precious!

> For the love of Christ constraineth [compels] us; because we thus judge, that if One died for all, then were all dead: And that He died for all, that they which live should not henceforth live unto themselves, but unto Him which died for them, and rose again (II Corinthians 5:14-15).

As I'm learning to yield myself, abandon myself to Him, I'm coming to know a joy that only He can give. Of course I'm far from perfect, and I still have so much to learn. Nevertheless, as I have surrendered this body which He bought with a price (I Corinthians 6:19-20) to allow Him to live His life in and through me, I've seen His power at work. When He is in control of my body, He is using me as His eyes and ears and mouth and hands and feet—they are His instruments that He can use to reach out and touch hearts with His love and truth.

Before I speak to any ladies' group I have to pray, "Lord, I have nothing to say to them because I have no idea what they need. But You do. You know everything, and You have the power to change their lives. Please say through me what You want to say and accomplish Your purpose in the lives of these ladies that You love so dearly."

When I do abandon my body to Him, He does such marvellous things. Just the other day a woman came to a retreat where I spoke about many of the truths we've been exploring.

She had been depressed and even suicidal, but the Lord gave her answers and hope. I was able to spend some additional time with her, using God's Word to deal with specific problems and needs. What a joy it was for me to see the peace and joy that came into her heart! "I" certainly couldn't help her, but as I yielded to His control, the Lord could include me in the wonderful joy of His working in her life.

When I see the Lord working in such ways, I can't help but think of something that happened to me over twenty years ago, not long after I was saved. I was attending a wedding and the pastor was giving the challenge to the bride and groom for their marriage. At the same time the Lord was challenging me, asking me if I would be willing, if He wanted me to, to stay single for the rest of my life and just have Him as my Bridegroom. I said "yes" to Him that day, not fully understanding, but wanting His best for my life.

Right after that the Lord in an amazing way took out of my life the Christian guy I was seriously dating at the time. But at the same time He gave me repeated assurances that He could be everything I needed in my life. It was like the Lord was saying, "Yes, Wilma, I can meet every need in your life and fulfill you in a way that no man ever could. You are *My bride!"*

> Wherefore, my brethren, ye also are become dead to
> the law by the body of Christ; that ye should be married
> to another, even to Him who is raised from the dead,
> that we should bring forth fruit unto God (Romans 7:4).

As you can imagine, this verse from Romans is very real and personal to me. But it is no less true for any Christian— married or single, man or woman. We belong to Christ, and He wants to be our All in All. And in addition, we are to bear fruit for Him. This, too, has special meaning for me because I'll never have physical children of my own. Yet I can have thousands of children in the Lord as I allow His Spirit to touch the lives of other people through me. I just always pray that the children look more like their Father than their mother!

You know, when a woman is pregnant there is a glow in her countenance that's not there normally. I guess it's caused by hormonal changes, but most of you know what I'm talking about. In a similar way, there's a glow that comes about each of us as we allow our Lord to work through us reproducing His life in others. What a joy it is to feel that glow! What a thrill it is to have people say that they see Jesus in you!

Christ is exactly what I want people to see in my ministry—not Wilma. I don't have the answers. I want them to see Christ in me because that's the hope of glory for me and for them, too (Colossians 1:27). The last thing I want to hear from ladies as they walk out of my meetings is, "Boy, she sure was funny!" or "Boy, that was a fun retreat!" Instead, I want them saying, "I saw a difference in her, and I want to be different, too!"

I want to be "salt" and "light." I want to be "salt" to make people thirsty for Jesus Christ so that they'll come, taste, and see that the Lord is good (Psalm 34:8). I want to be a "light" shining in the darkness, letting people know that they don't have to live in spiritual darkness any longer. They can have the "Light of life" (John 8:12), Who not only paid for the penalty of their sin but also has given them the power over sin in their lives.

> He giveth power to the faint; and to them that have no might He increaseth strength. . . . But they that wait upon the LORD shall renew their strength; they shall mount up with wings as eagles; they shall run, and not be weary; and they shall walk, and not faint (Isaiah 40:29, 31).

I often say that I don't have a religion any more; I have a very personal relationship with my precious Lord. And that blessed relationship with Him naturally gives me a desire to live for and to serve Him. Thankfully, trusting in the sovereignty and all-sufficiency of our God, we don't have to muster up our own energy and our own will-power to do what we think He wants us to do. When we try to do it ourselves, all of our service is self-centered. But because of our relationship with Him, God Himself works His will through us!

We should have the humble and obedient attitude of Christ (Philippians 2:5-8), who said, "the Son *can do nothing of Himself,* but what He seeth the Father do" (John 5:19). *"I can of Mine own Self do nothing* . . . because I seek not Mine own will, but the will of the Father which hath sent Me" (John 5:30). And also, *"I do nothing of Myself,* but as My Father hath taught Me, I speak these things. And He that sent Me is with Me: the Father hath not left Me alone; for I do always those things that please Him" (John 8:28-29).

> As the living Father hath sent Me, and I live by the Father: so he that eateth Me, even he shall *live by Me* (John 6:57).

The above passage comes from Christ's presentation of Himself as the "Bread of Life." Spiritually, we take Him in at salvation so that He may be the very sustenance of our lives. The point, then, is that we live by—because of and through the power of—Christ. And so what we do is not to be of ourselves but of His will and His leading. This abandonment to Him frees us from the futility of serving Him in our own strength.

When we try, try, try in our own strength, we often "burnout." Burn out is so common in Christian work because we try to accomplish God's work in our own flesh. But when we serve Him with His strength in the power of the Holy Spirit, He will work in us "to will and to do of His good pleasure" (Philippians 2:13). It's not that our bodies will never get tired, but that we will know and experience in our labors the reality of God's sustaining power. He increases our strength so that we can "mount up with wings as eagles."

His constraining love motivates us and takes the "have to's" out of doing what He calls us to do and makes them "want to's." There is a joyful abandonment to Him to be used wherever, whenever, and however He chooses, because we know that all is for His glory and the good of the people with whom we have to do for Him.

I've sensed Him at work in this way often in the past few years. Ladies come up to me after I've spoken at a meeting, and have said, "I've been asking the Lord to teach me this . . ." [whatever the point might have been], "and He has brought you here to say just exactly what I needed to hear in answer to my prayers!" What a joy!

I know the Lord has given me a unique ministry, but you can't look at me or anyone else and think that the Lord won't work through you like that. All of the people God has placed in your life—your family members, your friends and neighbors, your co-workers, your church family—each one is an opportunity for the Lord to use you. Let Him be sovereign and all-sufficient in your life. Let Him use His instruments—your eyes, your ears, your mouth, your hands, your feet—to touch their hearts and meet their needs.

But I need to add a word of caution here. Don't ever concentrate on being useful to the Lord. When, how, and how much He uses us is His business. If we concentrate on those things and we *think* we are not being used, we worry and fret and get everything out of order. Or, if we focus on ways we *think* we are being used, we will become proud, and then we will be resisted by Him (James 4:6).

Instead we must concentrate on Him. We will be useful if we are focusing on Him (Ephesians 2:10). And it is while experiencing that most blessed fellowship and communion with Him that we lose our lives and find them in our dear Savior. There is light and joy and blessing while walking with Him, listening to Him, and ever wanting to know Him more deeply and fully.

That most important point of really wanting *to know* my Lord is exactly what He brought to my attention back in 1991 when in brokenness I fell before Him. It was as if He was saying to me, "Wilma, you know many of My words from Scripture. You know countless guidelines for living a Christian life. But Wilma, you don't know Me! It's not your busy service. It's not even your strictly pure behavior that I want. It's your heart's desire to know Me! My power gives you *'all things* that pertain unto life and godliness, *through the knowledge of Me"* (II Peter 1:3).

> Thou wilt shew me the path of life: in Thy presence is *fullness of joy;* at Thy right hand there are pleasures for evermore (Psalm 16:11).

Our Lord's path is the path of life, not just for salvation, but for every moment of our earthly walk. Realizing His life in us and knowing His presence in us—that is the very source of "fullness of joy" for us. Sorrows and griefs may come, but that deep joy of acknowledging and finding our life in the presence of our indwelling Savior abides with us.

Nehemiah 8:10 tells us "The joy of the LORD is your strength." A joyless Christianity is pitifully weak, and unfortunately we live among many joyless and weak Christians. We can look everywhere for answers to the problems, but as I've come to learn, the only place where we will find true joy to strengthen us is in the presence of our dear Lord. Continuously recognizing and surrendering to His life in us allows His Spirit to bring forth His most desirable fruit in our lives—love, *joy,* peace, . . . (Galatians 5:22). And the joy of His presence will be our strength.

> Rejoice in the Lord alway: and again I say, Rejoice (Philippians 4:4).

We as Christians have so much cause to rejoice in our wonderful Savior and Lord. As we come to know Him, we find that He is everything we need—our Way, our Truth, our very Life—"Whom having not seen, [we] love; in whom, though now [we] see Him not, yet believing, [we] rejoice with *joy unspeakable and full of glory!"* (I Peter 1:8).

To know God as our "exceeding joy" is to know and embrace Christ as our life. We surrender our own wills and ways, giving up all our rights to Him. We admit our total weakness to claim only His strength. We recognize His sovereignty and rest in the fact that all of our cares are safely in His *a Song for Winter*

all-sufficient hands. It's not our life—it's His. What a glorious surrender! What a joyful abandon!

I SURRENDER ALL

All to Jesus I surrender, All to Him I freely give;
I will ever love and trust Him, In His presence daily live.

All to Jesus I surrender, Humbly at His feet I bow,
Worldly pleasures all forsaken, Take me, Jesus, take me now.

All to Jesus I surrender, Make me, Savior, wholly Thine;
Let me feel the Holy Spirit,—Truly know that Thou art mine.

All to Jesus I surrender, Lord, I give myself to Thee;
Fill me with Thy love and power, Let Thy blessing fall on me.

I surrender all, I surrender all.
All to Thee, my blessed Savior, I surrender all.

Judson W. Van DeVenter
1896

1. Are your daily needs, which God promises to know and meet, the focus of your attention rather than knowing Him? See Matthew 6:30-33.

2. Is the Lord sovereign and all-sufficient in your life?

3. Do your eyes, your ears, your mouth, your hands, your feet, and your mind belong to God for Him to use as His instruments?

4. Would the word "abandon" characterize your Christian life? How about "joyful"?

Epilogue

Sing unto Him, sing psalms unto Him, talk ye of all His won-drous works. Glory ye in His holy name; let the heart of them rejoice that seek the LORD. Seek the LORD and His strength, seek His face continually.

(I CHRONICLES 16:9-11)

In every season of our lives, the Lord is our Song. He is our salvation and our very life. When we come to Him with a bro-ken spirit, emptied of pride and self-will, we find Him as our forgiving and compassionate Deliverer. We find that our hopes are fulfilled in Him and that He is our Rock in whom we can trust. In Him we find perfect peace and wondrous love. We are washed clean and pure in His holiness, and abiding in Him we find real contentment and sweet rest. Oh may we be joyfully abandoned to His will.

He is our Song, and the themes of His goodness and grace abound. Let's continue to explore and enjoy them for a lifetime and let them compose an anthem of glorious praise to our great Savior.

As I talk to ladies everywhere, I often remind them of what Paul told the Corinthians: "We have this treasure [the light of the glorious gospel of Christ] in earthen vessels, that the excellency of the power may be of God, and not of us" (II Corinthians 4:7). And our part is to keep our "vessels" cleansed so that they may be vessels "unto honour, sanctified, and meet for the Master's use, and prepared unto every good work" (II Timothy 2:21).

I want to leave you with the thoughts of a song I've claimed as the theme for my life and ministry. May these words be a true reflection of our heart's prayer to God for our lives.

Epilogue

CHANNELS ONLY

How I praise Thee, precious Saviour,
That Thy love laid hold of me;
Thou hast saved and cleansed and filled me
That I might Thy channel be.

Emptied that Thou shouldest fill me,
A clean vessel in Thy hand;
With no power but as Thou givest
Graciously with each command.

Witnessing Thy power to save me,
Setting free from self and sin;
Thou who boughtest to possess me,
In Thy fullness, Lord, come in.

Jesus, fill now with Thy Spirit
Hearts that full surrender know;
That the streams of living water
From our inner man may flow.

Channels only, blessed Master,
But with all Thy wondrous pow'r
Flowing thro' us, Thou canst use us
Ev'ry day and ev'ry hour.

Mary E. Maxwell
Copyright, 1910, by May Agnew Stephens

A Personal Invitation

If after reading this book you realize that you have never accepted God's free gift of eternal life—or if you simply are not sure that you are in Christ—I invite you to receive Him right now. In my early years, I didn't know that going to heaven is a free gift. I always thought that I had to believe all the facts about Jesus and that I also had to do things to work my way to heaven. However God said in His Word that it's "not by works of righteousness which we have done, but according to His mercy He saved us, by the washing of regeneration, and renewing of the Holy Ghost; which He shed on us abundantly through Jesus Christ our Saviour" (Titus 3:5-6). God also said, "For by grace are ye saved through faith; and that not of yourselves: it is the gift of God: not of works, lest any man should boast" (Ephesians 2:8-9).

Salvation is a free gift that you accept by faith. A suggested prayer for asking Jesus Christ for His forgiveness and free gift of eternal life is:

> Lord Jesus, thank You for dying in my place on the cross to pay the penalty for my sins. Please forgive me and give me Your free gift of salvation. As a new, born-again child of God, please teach me more about Your love and grace and about my relationship with You. Take my life and make me into the person You want me to be. Amen.

If you have received Jesus Christ through reading this book or if you would like more information, I would appreciate hearing from you. May God bless you with a deep personal understanding and experience of His matchless love, grace, and mercy!

Wilma Sullivan
P. O. Box 16734
Greenville, SC 29606

Scripture Index

Genesis
41:51-52 – p. 71
45:5 – p. 73
50:19-20 – p. 73

Deuteronomy
33:27 – p. 48

I Samuel
13:14 – p. 28

II Samuel
12:7 – p. 28

I Chronicles
16:9-11 – pp. 16, 135

Nehemiah
8:10 – p. 131

Psalms
9:9-10 – pp. 55
16:11 – pp. 30, 44, 131
32:7-9 – p. 33
33:1-5 – p. 89
34: 3 – p. iii
34:8 – p. 128
34:14 – p. 73
37:4 – p. 101
37:5-7 – p. 120
38:1-18 – p. 69
40:2-3 – pp. viii, 51
40:8 – p. 125
42:1-2 – p. 14
42:8 – p. 115
43:4 – p. 123
46:1 – p. 55
46:10 – pp. 55, 115
51:10-17 – pp. 23, 28, 31
62:5 – p. 105
63:1-5 – pp. 14, 107
91:14-16 – p. 40
95:7b-11 – pp. 25, 26
96:1-2 – p. 11

103:14 – p. 80
104:33-34 – p. 123
119:11 – p. 52
132:9 – p. 123
139:1-2 – p. 29
139: 7-10 – p. 47
139:23-24 – pp. 28, 29, 32

Proverbs
3:5-6 – pp. 51, 52
3:11-12 – p. 85
13:10 – p. 68
23:7 – pp. 72, 75

Isaiah
12:2-5 – pp. viii, 3
26:3-4 – pp. 59, 66, 116
30:15 – p. 119
30:21 – p. 116
40:29, 31 – p. 128
41:10 – p. 57
57:15 – p. 28
64:6 – p. 90
66:2b – p. 24

Jeremiah
9:23-24 – pp. 14, 81-82
17:9-10a – pp. 29, 68
29:13-14 – p. 15
31:3 – pp. 81, 85

Ezekiel
16:1-15 – p. 24, 25

Habakkuk
2:4 – p. 120

Zephaniah
3:17 – pp. 77, 85

Matthew
6:14-15 – p. 70
6:30-33 – pp. 124, 133
9:13 – p. 6

scripture index